THE WEB WIZARD'S GUIDE TO DREAMWEAVER

D1515468

JAMES G. LENGEL

PEARSON

Addison
Wesley

Boston   San Francisco   New York
London   Toronto   Sydney   Tokyo   Singapore   Madrid
Mexico City   Munich   Paris   Cape Town   Hong Kong   Montreal

Senior Acquisitions Editor: *Michael Hirsch*
Project Editor: *Maite Suarez-Rivas*
Senior Production Supervisor: *Juliet Silveri*
Marketing Manager: *Nathan Schultz*
Senior Marketing Coordinator: *Lesly Hershman*
Production Supervision: *Kathy Smith*
Cover and Interior Designer: *Leslie Haimes*
Composition: *Gillian Hall, The Aardvark Group*
Copyeditor: *Kathy Smith*
Proofreader: *Holly McLean-Aldis*
Text and Cover Design Supervisor: *Gina Hagen Kolenda/Joyce Cosentino Wells*
Print Buyer: *Caroline Fell*

Access the latest information about Addison-Wesley titles from our World Wide Web site: *http://www.aw.com/computing*

Many of the designations used by manufacturers and sellers to distinguish their products are claimed as trademarks. Where those designations appear in this book, and Addison-Wesley was aware of a trademark claim, the designations have been printed in initial caps or all caps.

The programs and applications presented in this book have been included for their instructional value. They have been tested with care, but are not guaranteed for any particular purpose. The publisher does not offer any warranties or representations, not does it accept any liabilities with respect to the programs or applications.

Library of Congress Cataloging-in-Publication Data
Lengel, James G.
   The Web Wizard's Guide to Dreamweaver / James G. Lengel
      p. cm.
   Includes index.
   ISBN 0-321-14265-9
   1. Dreamweaver (Computer file) 2. Web sites--Design. I. Title

   TK5105.8885.D74L45 2004
   005.7'2—dc22   2003062409

2345678910—QWT—0504

TABLE OF CONTENTS

PREFACE

About Addison-Wesley's Web Wizard Series

The beauty of the Web is that, with a little effort, anyone can harness its power to create sophisticated Web sites. *Addison-Wesley's Web Wizard Series* helps readers master the Web by presenting a concise introduction to one important Internet topic or technology in each book. The books start from square one and assume no prior experience with the technology being covered. Mastering the Web doesn't come with a wave of a magic wand, but by studying these accessible, highly visual textbooks, readers will be well on their way.

The series is written by instructors familiar with the challenges beginners face when first learning the material. To this end, the Web Wizard books offer more than a cookbook approach: they emphasize principles and offer clear explanations, giving the reader a strong foundation of knowledge on which to build.

Numerous features highlight important points and aid in learning:

☆ Tips—important points to keep in mind

☆ Shortcuts—time-saving ideas

☆ Warnings—things to watch out for

☆ Review questions and hands-on exercises

☆ Online references—Web sites to visit for more information

Supplements

Supplementary materials for the books, including updates, additional examples, and source code are available at `http://www.aw-bc.com/webwizard`. Also available for instructors adopting a book from the series are instructors' manuals, test banks, PowerPoint slides, solutions, and Course Compass—a dynamic online course management system powered by Blackboard. Please contact your sales representative for the instructor resources access code.

About This Book

This book is an introduction to using Dreamweaver for Web site development. No previous programming experience is required, although prior experience working with HTML is helpful. The book is a visual learning tool for students and developers. It uses dozens of diagrams to illustrate different Dreamweaver techniques.

The book also contains a wealth of end-of-chapter review material with many questions and hands-on assignments derived from actual classroom assignments and projects. Since skill levels can vary greatly, many hands-on exercises have optional portions that vary in level of difficulty. If you are reading this book without taking a class, try one or two hands-on exercises in each chapter to apply the material. Like learning to ride a bike, the best way to learn a new language is to practice.

Acknowledgments

I'd like to thank the thousands of students who built their first Web sites with Dreamweaver in the labs at the College of Communication at Boston University, whose work provided the impetus for this book. Thanks are also due to the family members who watched me ignore them as I wrote the chapters of this book.

In addition, the book reviewers offered many great ideas and comments that truly made this a better book. These reviewers include

Daniel Bogaard, Rochester Institute of Technology

Michelle C. Heckman

Renee Human, Lexington Community College

Michael J. Hutchinson

Mary A. Kincaid, Caldwell Community College and Technical Institute

Jane Mackay, Texas Christian University

Anita Philipp, Oklahoma City Community College

Rick Warkenthien, Southeast Technical Institute

James G. Lengel
October 2003

CHAPTER ONE

INTRODUCTION TO DREAMWEAVER

 ## Survey the Vessel

This chapter introduces Dreamweaver and gets you started building a basic Web site. Along the way, you will become familiar with the Dreamweaver development environment, learn the difference between Dreamweaver and HTML, and be introduced to some of the tools that Dreamweaver provides Web site authors.

In harbors all around the country, you will find sailboats with the name *Dream Weaver* stenciled across the transom. Before these boats set off, the skipper surveys the vessel to learn the ropes and make sure the ship is well-found. This chapter provides a survey of the computer software also called Dreamweaver, which you may think of as the vessel in which you will set forth on your journey across the World Wide Web.

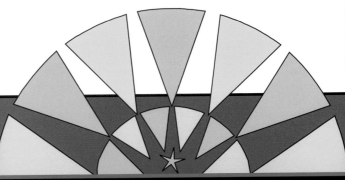

◎◎ Chapter Objectives

☆ Learn the nature of Dreamweaver, and understand why and when it should be used

☆ Understand the difference between building a Web page with Dreamweaver and programming a page with HyperText Markup Language (HTML)

☆ Learn the basic elements of the Dreamweaver development environment

☆ Build a simple Web page with Dreamweaver

◎◎ What Is Dreamweaver? Why Use It?

The Importance of Being an Author

Few people would consider publishing their own newspaper, producing their own television show, or printing their own book. But it seems that everyone wants to display a Web site on the Internet. Unlike the mass media that preceded it, the Internet offers the opportunity for each of us to be an author as well as a reader, a producer as well as a consumer, and a sender as well as a receiver of information and ideas.

To author a book, you need a special set of tools: a pen or word processor to compose with, a computer to lay out the pages, a press to print the pages, and a binder to assemble the book. To author a Web site, you need a different set of tools:

☆ a word processor for writing your text

☆ a window to import and display your images, sound, and video

☆ tools to make buttons, boxes, and text fields for the viewer to make choices and enter data

☆ layout tools for designing and formatting the pages

☆ a method for turning all of this into the HTML code the Web understands

☆ tools for sending your pages to a Web server

Dreamweaver provides all of these tools, and more. Without these tools, most people would not be able to create and publish their own Web pages.

> ☆ **TIP   Authoring vs. Surfing**
>
> If all you want to do is surf the Web—looking at pages that have been posted by others—then you don't need Dreamweaver, and you don't need this book. This guide is for people who want to publish their own information and ideas on the Web. Dreamweaver helps you make the waves that others will surf upon.

Every page on the Web, from your uncle Fred's personal Web page to the thousand-page sites of major companies, was authored by someone. Not all of them used Dreamweaver, but most of them used something like it. Dreamweaver is one of the most comprehensive and most popular tools for authoring on the Web.

Why Dreamweaver?

You don't need Dreamweaver to author a Web page. You could write your page directly in HTML code. You could use another authoring program such as Microsoft FrontPage, Netscape Composer, or Adobe GoLive. You could develop your pages in Flash, Shockwave, or JavaScript. You could go to a Web site such as SiteRightNow (`http://www.siterightnow.net/index.html`), enter a few bits of information, and watch it create a Web page for you. Of all of these choices, Dreamweaver is for most people the easiest, most comprehensive, and most effective way to author a Web site.

The developers at Macromedia created Dreamweaver as a program easy enough to be used by a beginning Web author, but comprehensive enough to be used by a professional Webmaster. Macromedia's expertise lies in the development of multimedia authoring tools such as Director, Flash, SoundEdit, and Authorware. These programs have been used for decades by programmers and non-programmers alike to create and publish multimedia CD-ROMs and Web sites.

In 1996, programmers at Macromedia set out to apply their know-how to the development of a WYSIWYG Web-authoring tool. The result was Dreamweaver, now in its sixth edition, and used by thousands around the world.

> ☆ **TIP** **WYSIWYG (What You See Is What You Get)**
>
> WYSIWYG is a way of describing how Dreamweaver works. As you develop your Web page in Dreamweaver, what you see in the Dreamweaver window is very much like what viewers will see in their Web browsers when they visit your site.

Dreamweaver is much easier to learn than HTML, JavaScript, or Flash. To create a multi-page, interactive, multimedia Web site with Dreamweaver will take less time and require less programming than any of these other methods. Dreamweaver is more universal than FrontPage, which is designed to work best with Microsoft servers and browsers; the Web sites FrontPage creates don't always translate well to other platforms. Dreamweaver is much more comprehensive than Netscape Composer, and allows you to create and manage more complex sites that are rich with media. While Dreamweaver may cost a bit more than some of these other programs, its combination of completeness and ease of use make it the best choice for a beginning Web author.

What Dreamweaver Is (and Isn't)

Dreamweaver is a Web page editor and Web site manager. It provides all the tools you need to assemble a Web page that contains text, images, sound, video, animation, links, and forms. It also supplies tools for assembling a large collection of Web pages into a coordinated Web site, and for posting this site to a Web server. But it does not provide tools for creating multimedia: images, sound, video, or animations. These kinds of media must be created outside of Dreamweaver, with other software tools.

Most Web developers combine Dreamweaver with other tools as they build their Web sites. Table 1.1 shows some of these tools and what they do.

Table 1.1 Media Types and Editing Tools

Media Type	Typical Software Program
Images	Adobe Photoshop, Photoshop Elements. PaintShop Pro, Macromedia Fireworks
Sound	Macromedia SoundEdit, CoolEdit Pro, SoundForge, Peak, Deck
Video	Final Cut Pro, iMovie, Adobe Premiere, QuickTime Player Pro, Windows MovieMaker
Animation	Macromedia Flash, GIF Animator, GIFBuilder, Fireworks
Web-Linked Databases	FileMaker Pro, Cold Fusion

As you build a Web page, especially one with multimedia, you will need to use some of these other programs along with Dreamweaver. For instance, you might use Photoshop to download an image from your digital camera and then to edit the image to the proper size and resolution for your Web page. And you might use Flash to create an animated banner ad for your site. Once you have created the image and animation files in these other programs, you may import these files into Dreamweaver and place them on your Web page.

Dreamweaver cannot download pictures from your digital camera, record sound, or edit images. You must use other programs to prepare these kinds of files for your Web site. Dreamweaver provides tools for editing and formatting text, but not for editing and formatting the other media commonly used on the Web. As this book covers each type of media in the following chapters, you will learn the best ways to prepare multimedia files for use in Dreamweaver.

Dreamweaver is not a Web server. It cannot deliver your files over the Internet directly to other Web users. It also cannot turn your computer into a Web server. When you complete the process of building your Web site with Dreamweaver, you need to send the site to a Web server in order for it to be available to others online. Dreamweaver provides tools to help you send your site to the server, but cannot be a server itself.

☆**TIP** **The Skillet**

Think of Dreamweaver as a skillet, in which you combine and cook the elements of a meal. Before you put the skillet on the fire, you prepare the various food items by peeling and slicing them with tools specially designed for those purposes—you wouldn't chop a pepper with the skillet. Once prepared, you use the skillet to mix the elements together and to change their form and taste through cooking. And when you are done, you don't serve the meal to the diners in the skillet—they use their own plates and knives and forks to actually consume the meal. Think of Photoshop and the other media programs as the choppers and slicers, and think of the user's Web browser as the dinner plate.

The best way to use Dreamweaver—and the way this book is written—is to use it in combination with the other software programs that help prepare the various media elements.

How to Get Dreamweaver

There are many ways to obtain a copy of Dreamweaver to use as you work through this book:

☆ You can buy Dreamweaver at your local computer store or bookstore.

☆ You can buy it over the Web from a variety of online vendors. You can find a list of vendors at
`http://www.macromedia.com/buy/volume_license/`
`corp_resellers.html`

☆ You can buy it online directly from Macromedia at
`http://www.macromedia.com/store`. If you are a student or faculty member at a school or college, you can take advantage of an educational discount that brings the price of Dreamweaver below $100.

☆ You can download a free trial copy from the Macromedia Web site at
`http://www.macromedia.com/downloads`.

☆ You can install it from a site license CD or server at your school or company. Macromedia offers a volume purchase program that reduces the cost of each copy.

Dreamweaver is available for the Windows 98, 2000, NT, ME, or XP operating systems, and also for the Apple Macintosh systems 9 and 10. The current version as this book is written is Dreamweaver MX, but most of the instructions here will also apply (with a few changes) to Dreamweaver 4.

Once purchased, you must install the software on your computer. Don't just copy the files; launch the installation program that Macromedia provides. This will ensure that all of the parts of Dreamweaver that you need are installed in the right places on your computer. Dreamweaver is a large and complex program that contains a rich set of resources that must be available as you use it.

◎◎ Dreamweaver vs. HTML

A Web page can be built in many different ways: by using a WYSIWYG page editor such as Dreamweaver, GoLive, or FrontPage; by writing the HTML code directly; by writing JavaScript code; or developing in Flash or Shockwave. Many Web developers swear that their favorite method is the best (or only) way to develop a Web page. You might have heard someone claim, "I never use WYSIWYG editors like Dreamweaver. I develop all my Web pages directly in HTML. Real programmers write code directly." Here's what it means.

All standard Web pages are stored in HTML (HyperText Markup Language), even those developed with Dreamweaver. HTML is the code that Web browsers such as Explorer and Netscape need in order to operate. (They can also read JavaScript code, but this is almost always embedded in an HTML file.) This code contains the instructions that the browser needs in order to display the Web page to the viewer. For instance, the HTML code for today's *Financial Times* Web page begins like this:

```
<!DOCTYPE HTML PUBLIC "-//W3C//DTD HTML 4.01 Transitional//EN">
<html>
<head>
<meta http-equiv="Content-Type" content="text/html;
   charset=iso-8859-1"/>
<script> var showSubPage='N';
</script>
<script language=JavaScript type="text/javascript">
var CommonTemplateVersion=1.0;
var FTSection='1hom';
var FTPage='1homepg';
var FTSite=getValue('FTSite','FTCOM');
var FTIndustry = 'XXXX';
var AssetType='Page';
var PageTitle='Home US';
function getValue(key,defaultVal)
{var value=defaultVal;var ck=typeof
   location.search!='undefined'?location.search.toString():'';
   var begin;var str;
   if(key&&key.length>0&&ck&&ck.length>0)
{key+='=';begin=ck.indexOf(key)>-1?ck.indexOf(key)+key.length:-1;
   if(begin>-1)
{str=ck.substr(begin,ck.length);value=str.substr(0,str.indexOf('&')
   >0?str.indexOf('&'):str.length);}} return(value);}
</script>
...
</head>
<body bgcolor=white vlink="#333333" link="#333333" leftmargin="0"
   topmargin="0" marginheight="0" marginwidth="0"
   onload="commonOnLoad()">
<table cellpadding=0 cellspacing="0" border="0" width="772">
<tr>
<td><img src="/c.gif" width="6" height="1"></td>
<td bgcolor="#990000"><img src="/c.gif" width="134" height="1"></td>
<td bgcolor="#990000"><img src="/c.gif" width="15" height="1"></td>
<td bgcolor="#990000"><img src="/c.gif" width="468" height="1"></td>
<td bgcolor="#990000"><img src="/c.gif" width="15" height="1"></td>
<td bgcolor="#003399"><img src="/c.gif" width="134" height="1"></td>
... ...
```

. . . and goes on like this for more than ten single-spaced pages of dense code—just to display a single Web page. To learn to write this code from scratch takes a long time. To edit a page by adjusting this code is not easy, especially for a beginner. This same page in Dreamweaver would look like Figure 1.1.

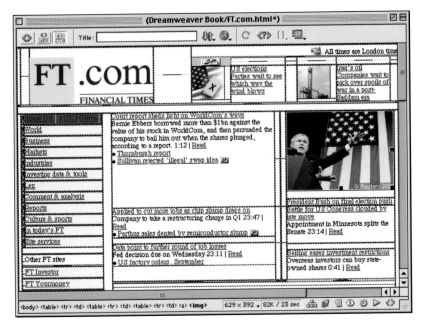

Figure 1.1   Financial Times Page in Dreamweaver

As you can see, the Dreamweaver approach is quite different, and in some ways easier for a beginner (or even a seasoned professional) to work with and understand. Dreamweaver provides both the WYSIWYG view of the page and the code itself.

When Dreamweaver saves a Web page, it saves it in HTML code that looks just like the code sample shown above. As you assemble the elements of your page in Dreamweaver, it is creating the HTML code for you. Dreamweaver lets you assemble the page in an environment that displays the page as it will look to the viewer. But underneath it all Dreamweaver is creating standard HTML code for the browser. You may also write HTML code directly with Dreamweaver.

Figure 1.2 shows a diagram of the relationship of Dreamweaver to the HTML file, the server, and the viewer's browser. Dreamweaver lets you view the page in WYSIWYG form. When you save the page, it produces a text file that contains the HTML and other code that describes the page. This file is sent to a Web server, along with the other files that make up your site. When the viewer calls up your page, the server sends the HTML file. On the viewer's computer, the browser interprets this HTML code and displays the page to the viewer.

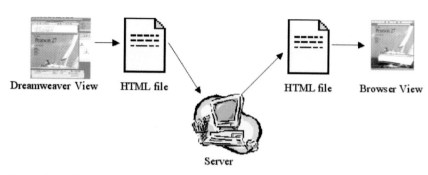

Figure 1.2   Dreamweaver, HTML, and the Browser

You can create hundreds of pages in Dreamweaver without ever looking at the HTML code. But if you want to see the code, it's there: Dreamweaver lets you see (and edit) the HTML if you want to. It is the best of both worlds. But for most beginners, the world that works best is the world of WYSIWYG editing.

◎◎ The Dreamweaver Development Environment

Dreamweaver allows you to set up an environment on your computer screen that contains a selection of windows and tools, within which you build your Web pages. A typical environment might look like Figure 1.3.

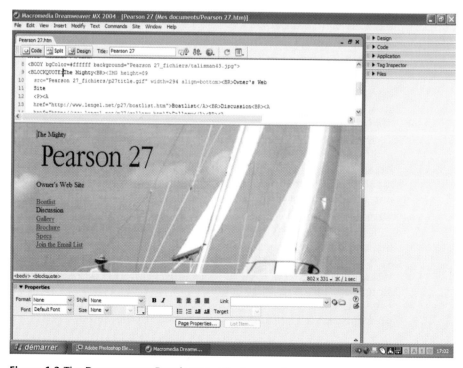

Figure 1.3 The Dreamweaver Development Environment

All Those Windows

The big window in the center is the document window. In this example, it is split into two parts, showing the HTML code at the top and the WYSIWYG view at the bottom. Below the document window is the Properties window, a very useful part of the environment that shows you the attributes of the item you are currently working on. In this example, it shows the properties of the text that is being edited. (If the image were selected, the Properties window would show information about the image. This window changes its nature depending on what is selected.)

> ☆ **WARNING   A Site of Many Files**
>
> A Web site is a complex publication that consists of many separate files. Each page of the site exists as its own HTML file. Each image is included as a separate JPEG or GIF file; each video, animation, and sound may be found in the site as other individual files. It's quite a chore to keep track of these files, name them properly, and organize them into folders, so Dreamweaver provides site management tools, such as the Site Map window, to help you keep track of all the files.

The menubar provides easy access to most of the functions and potential uses of Dreamweaver as well.

Seldom does a Web developer open all of Dreamweaver's windows at the same time. A typical working environment includes a few windows, as shown in Figure 1.2. But it's a good idea to realize the breadth all of the program's tools at the outset. Table 1.2 lists the program's windows, and what they do.

Table 1.2   Dreamweaver's Windows and What They Do

Window	What It Does
Editing	Displays the page, its HTML code, or both
Properties	Shows the properties of the selected item in the Document window; provides tools to modify those properties
Insert	Provides icons that let you insert various items into the page, from text to tables to forms to scripts
Design	Lets you apply HTML and CSS (Cascading Style Sheet) styles and add various behaviors to your pages
Code	Lets you inspect the HTML code of your page, add common snippets of code, and look up HTML tags
Applications	Provides tools for connecting your Web page to a database and other applications running on a Web server
Files	Provides a list of files in your site and other commonly used files
Answers	Provides tutorials for learning to use Dreamweaver
Site	Shows a diagram of your site and a list of its files
Frames	Shows the way that this page uses frames (if any)

The menubar is also an important part of the Dreamweaver development environment. It's a good idea to look at these menus at the beginning of your work with Dreamweaver, so that you might know where to find the command you need. Table 1.3 shows the menu items and what they accomplish.

Table 1.3   Dreamweaver's Menus and What They Do

Menu	What It Does
File	Lets you open and save files; print the HTML code; import certain types of files; preview and check pages in a Web browser. It also shows a list of recently edited files.
Edit	Lets you cut, copy, paste, and clear; find and replace text in the page or in its code; format the appearance of the code; and set Dreamweaver's preferences
View	Adjusts the way your page looks as you edit it; lets you choose to see the design, the code, or both; and allows you to hide and show various editing features such as rulers, grids, and invisible items
Insert	Lets you insert items onto your Web page, such as images, sounds, animations, videos, forms, frames, anchors, special characters, and other objects
Modify	Lets you modify the properties of the entire page or of a selected item; create or modify a link; arrange layers; or apply a template style to your page
Text	Lets you modify the properties of selected text, including size, font, color, style, indentation, alignment, paragraph format; the spelling checker is also here
Commands	Lets you record and execute macros; format the HTML code; set up a slide show; format and sort a table of data; and set up a color scheme for the page
Site	Lets you access the site map, set up and define your site, manage the files in your site, analyze your HTML code, and change links throughout the site
Window	Opens and closes the various windows provided by Dreamweaver, as shown in Table 1.2
Help	Lets you access Dreamweaver help, tutorials, references, and online support

Menus, Windows, and Keyboard Shortcuts

Many of the tasks that you commonly perform with Dreamweaver can be accomplished by selecting from a menu item or from a window—the choice is yours. In this book, for the sake of simplicity and consistency, we will use the menu items wherever possible. The commands will be written in the form "Choose Text➔Style➔Bold from the menubar." You can accomplish the same result by clicking the little "B" button on the right side of the Properties window, but explaining it this way is subject to more misinterpretation. You can also do this by pressing ⌘+B (Macintosh) or Ctrl+B (Windows) from the keyboard. As you improve in your facility with Dreamweaver, you will develop your own style for using these commands, and decide for yourself whether to use the menus, the windows, or the keyboard shortcuts. Most beginners find the menu items a good starting point, so this book will provide menu item instructions wherever possible.

☆ **SHORTCUT** **Keyboard Shortcuts**

If you find yourself going back to the same menu item over and over, you might want to learn its keyboard shortcut. These shortcuts, if they exist, are shown in the menu item itself. Not all tasks and functions have keyboard shortcuts, but many of the common ones do.

As you move through this book, you will be introduced to many of the windows and menu items that Dreamweaver provides. You'll use them one by one as they become necessary. When a window is no longer needed, it's a good idea to close it, and keep the screen uncluttered. If you were to leave every window opened, the main document window would soon be buried and you'd find it hard to get your work done.

It's also a good idea to organize your windows in a consistent arrangement. This makes it easier and faster to work. The illustrations in this book will arrange the windows as shown in Figure 1.3, with the document window at the top center, the Properties window just below it, and other windows as necessary on the right.

Other Useful Tools

The Window Size tool is located at the bottom right edge of the document window. It shows the size of the window in which you are editing. This is an important set of numbers. If you design a page that's too big, it won't fit into the browsers your audience uses. If it is too small, it may not be able to contain the information your audience needs to see. Throughout this book, the Window Size will be set to 760 × 420 pixels, which is the space left inside the browser window for the typical Web viewer. The size to which you set the Dreamweaver Document window does not determine the size of the user's browser window; instead, it serves as a guide to you as you build your page.

The best way to get to know the Dreamweaver development environment is to work with it. In the next section of this chapter you will build a small Web site—nothing fancy or complicated, just enough to help you to understand how Dreamweaver works.

◎◎ Build a Web Page with Dreamweaver

The Web site that you will build in this introductory chapter is not meant to be a permanent professional piece of work. Think of it instead as a practice piece that you will assemble and experiment with simply to familiarize yourself with the Dreamweaver development environment. In Chapters Two through Eight of this book, you will more carefully build a permanent site.

Before you built a real Web site, you would carefully and deliberately determine the audience and purpose of your site. You would also develop a flow chart that sets forth the structure of the site, and sketch a design. Chapter Seven of this book will cover this process in more detail. You can also find detailed instructions on how to develop these planning documents in *The Web Wizard's Guide to Web Design*, by James G. Lengel.

For the purposes of this sample site, we'll assume you have done your planning and have these documents at hand. You will also need some media files to complete this exercise: a QuickTime video, a sound file, and a Flash animation. You can download sample media files for this exercise from the Web Wizard Web site. At the Web site, look for the *The Web Wizard's Guide to Dreamweaver*. In that section you will find a folder called *ch1sample* that contains a flow chart, a page design, and some media files. Download this folder to your computer, and you can use these files to complete this exercise.

Open Dreamweaver

Open Dreamweaver and arrange the windows as shown in Figure 1.3. Close any windows other than the Editing and Properties windows. Use the Window Size box at the bottom of the document window to set the size to 760×420 pixels. Choose View➔Design from the menubar to get the WYSIWYG view.

> ☆TIP   **Define Your Site**
>
> To get the most out of Dreamweaver, you should define the site, both conceptually and technically, before you begin to build it. It's not necessary to do this for the practice site in this chapter, but it would not hurt to do so. You will learn more about planning and defining your site in Chapter Seven. For now, if you'd like to define your site technically, choose Site➔Define Site from the menubar, and create a new site.

Insert Text

You will see the cursor flashing in the upper left corner of the page. Enter some text from the keyboard, or copy it from another source and paste it in. The text will appear in Dreamweaver's default font style and size. To change the appearance of the text, select it, and then use the items under the Text menu to modify the size, style, alignment, or color. To start a new paragraph, press the Return key. To start a new line, but not a new paragraph, press Shift+Return.

☆**TIP** **Where to Get Text and Other Materials**

The companion Web site to this book at http://www.aw-bc.com/webwizard contains some sample files for this project, which you may use in this exercise if you haven't got any of your own. You will find a text file (*hiyc.txt*), an image file (*boat.jpg*), a Flash animation (*hiyclogo.swf*), some music (*song.mov*), and a video clip (*shark.mov*). Download these files to a folder on your computer, and use them to build your sample in this chapter.

To make a headline, put the text on a line by itself, then set it to bold and to a larger size such as 5. To make a bulleted list, enter each bullet item as a new paragraph. Then select all the bullets, and choose Text→List→Unordered List from the menubar. To indent a paragraph, select it and then choose Text→Indent from the menubar.

As you can see, Dreamweaver here is working much like a word processor. The controls over text style, and the means of modifying it, are similar to those in Microsoft Word.

Too see what this page would look like to your audience, choose File→Preview in Browser→Internet Explorer (or Netscape Navigator).

☆**TIP** **Choose Your Browser**

Before you can preview your Web page in a browser, you need to tell Dreamweaver where your browsers are located. Choose File→Preview in Browser→Edit Browser List. Then use the "+" button to add a browser to the list. If you have both Internet Explorer and Netscape on your computer, add both of them to the list.

Notice that your page does not look exactly the same in the browser as it does in Dreamweaver. That's because the browser will interpret the page a bit differently than both Dreamweaver and other browsers. Your text may appear a little larger, or in a different font.

☆**WARNING** **Filenames**

Whenever you save a file that will be used in a Web site, you must take care to use a filename that will work well on the Web. Such filenames should contain only letters and numbers—no special characters and no spaces. They also must end with an appropriate filename extension—in this case, *.html* or *.htm*.

Insert enough text to make a simple Web page—perhaps two paragraphs. Then save the page. If you are using the sample files from the Web Wizard site, save the page into the *ch1sample* folder. If you are making your own sample site, create a new folder called *samplesite*, and save the file there.

Insert Images

Next, you'll add an image to your sample Web page. Before doing that, you need to prepare the image in the proper format. The images in the sample folder from the Web Wizard site—*boat.jpg* and *logo.gif*—are all set, but if you prepare your own image, you must make sure that it's saved in a proper form for the Web. If you are not sure of the format of your image, open it in a program like Photoshop or PaintShop Pro, and choose Save for Web from the File menu. Save it with a proper filename into the *ch1sample* or *samplesite* folder.

☆ **TIP** **Changing Filenames**

An image's filename must match its file type: A GIF image must end in .gif, and a JPEG in .jpg. But you can't change the file type simply by changing the filename extension. For example, to change an image from JPEG to GIF format, you need to open it in an image-editing program, and then choose the new format in the Save As dialog box.

Click the mouse to place the cursor at the point where you want the image to appear. Then choose Insert→Image from the menubar. Navigate to the image, click Open, and watch your image appear on the Web page. Your Web page may look something like Figure 1.4, containing some text and one image.

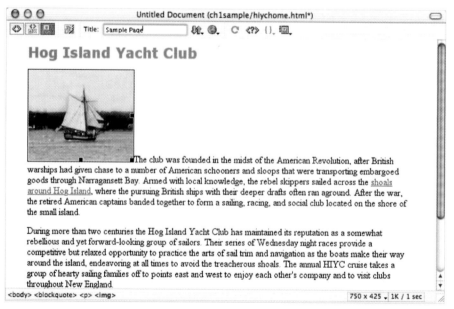

Figure 1.4 Web Page with Text and Image

The page might be more useful if the image were aligned to the left, with the text next to it on the right. To align the image to the left of the text, first select the image, then choose Align→Left from the popup menu at the lower right of the Properties window. Your page will now look something like Figure 1.5.

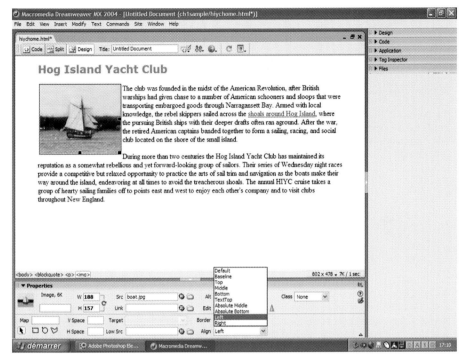

Figure 1.5 Web Page with Image Aligned Left

☆ **TIP**   **Concepts Now, Details Later**

At this point in the process of learning Dreamweaver, don't worry too much about the details of how the text or images look. This first chapter simply introduces you to the process of creating a Web page. Later chapters will cover the details of working with text, images, and other media. For now, work with the general concepts of construction, and save the details for later.

Save the page that now contains text and a picture.

Insert Multimedia

Most Web sites rely on text and images to carry the message to the audience, but in some cases, the user needs to hear a sound, see an animation, or watch a video clip to fully understand the content. These kinds of media are more difficult to prepare and more difficult to receive over the Web than their static counterparts. As you will learn in Chapter Four, multimedia may be used sparingly, and Dreamweaver can handle these media well.

Inserting a video, sound, or animation into a Web page works similarly to inserting an image. First, place your cursor at the point where you want the media to appear. Choose Insert→Media from the menubar, and then choose the type of media you want to insert.

To insert a Flash animation, for instance, choose Insert➔Media➔Flash from the menubar, and select a Flash (.swf) file. The animation will appear as a gray box in the Dreamweaver document window; you won't see the animation playing in Dreamweaver unless you click the green arrow in its Properties window.

☆**TIP** **Preparing Media Files**

Each type of media that you want to import into Dreamweaver—animation, video, and sound—must be prepared and saved in a format that works with Dreamweaver as well as the browsers of your audience. You will learn the rules on preparing the media files in Chapter Four, "Working with Multimedia." For now, you may use the files already prepared for you at the Web Wizard Web site.

To see the page with its animation, you must choose File➔Preview in Browser➔Internet Explorer (or Netscape Navigator) from the menubar. You can see what the sample animation looks like to the viewer in Figure 1.7.

☆**WARNING** **Plug-ins**

All of the multimedia types require browser plug-ins in order to work. For instance, without the Flash Player, your browser will not be able to display the sample animation that is part of this exercise. Text and images require no browser plug-ins, while animation, sound, and video do. Make sure you have the latest Flash and QuickTime plug-ins installed in your browser, so that you can try out these samples. You can download these for free at `http://www.macromedia.com`, and `http://www.apple.com/quicktime`.

To insert a sound on this page, place the cursor where you want the sound controller to appear. Then choose Insert➔Media➔Plugin from the menubar. Select the sound file, click Open, and watch as a small square grey plug-in icon appears, like Figure 1.6.

Figure 1.6 Plug-in Icon

To make the sound easier to control, stretch this icon out so that it's about 200 pixels wide. When the page displays in the browser, the icon will be replaced by a standard sound controller bar, as shown in Figure 1.7.

Before you add a video to your Web site, you should save the page you are working on and create a new page. It would be confusing to the viewer to see an animation, hear a sound, and watch a video all on the same page. To create a new page, choose File➔New from Dreamweaver's menubar, make sure Basic HTML page is selected, and then click the Create button. You will see a new Dreamweaver document window appear, with the text cursor blinking in the upper left corner. Enter a heading for this page, and add some text that explains the video.

Figure 1.7 Web Page with Animation and Sound in a Browser

To insert the video, place the cursor where you want the video to appear. Then choose Insert→Media→Plugin from the menubar. Select the video file, click Open, and watch as a small square grey plug-in icon appears, like the one shown in Figure 1.6. Stretch this icon out to fit the size of the video plus 16 pixels. The extra 16 pixels are for the controller bar. If you are using the sample video from the Web Wizard Web site, set the size of the plug-in icon to 160 pixels wide and 136 pixels high. It's easiest to enter these numbers directly into the Properties window for the video, as shown in Figure 1.8.

Preview this page in the browser. The video should play automatically, with a standard controller bar at the bottom. Save this second Web page with a proper filename. In this example, we'll call it *shoal.html*. Make sure you save it in the same folder as the other Web page.

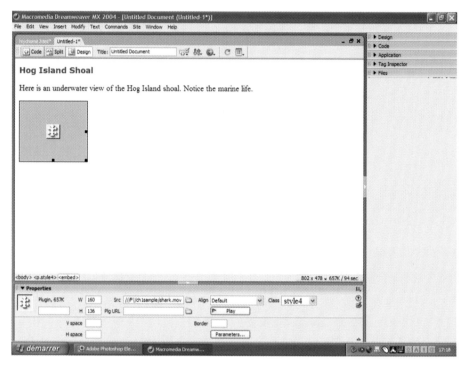

Figure 1.8 Setting the Size of the Video

Link the Pages

Your Web site now consists of two pages. You need to provide a way for the viewer to get from one page to another, with a hyperlink. Open the first page in Dreamweaver. Select a word or phrase to link from, as shown in Figure 1.9. Then choose Modify→Make Link from the menubar.

In the Select File dialog box, choose the file you want to link to. We are linking to the second page we made, which we named *shoal.html*, so we choose that file, as shown in Figure 1.10.

When the dialog box disappears, you will notice that the words you selected have turned blue. When clicked by the viewer in the browser, these words will link to the other Web page. Preview the page in your browser and try it.

You now have a Web site with two multimedia pages and a link. And you are finding your way around Dreamweaver, learning the ropes as you take this vessel on an introductory sail. You'll continue the voyage by adding a form and a rollover image.

> ☆ **WARNING** **Bells and Whistles**
>
> For many people, the practice Web page that you've built so far is sufficient for an introduction to Dreamweaver. The two sections that follow, on inserting a form, and on creating rollover buttons, may go beyond what you need to do at this point. They might be considered "bells and whistles," and can be left for a later time.

Build a Web Page with Dreamweaver

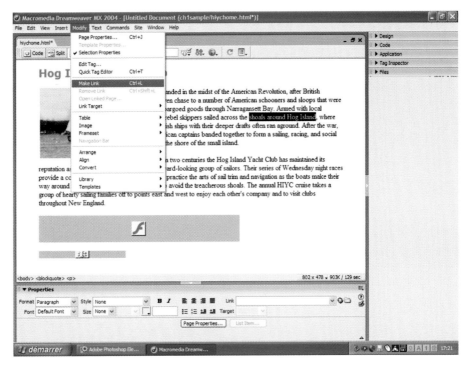

Figure 1.9 Making a Link from Selected Text

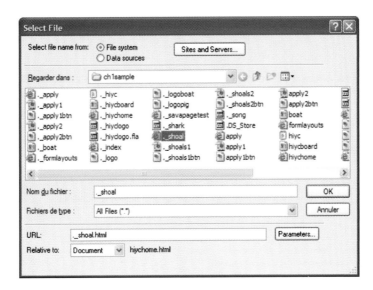

Figure 1.10 Choosing the File to Link to

Insert a Form

A form is a place on a Web page where the viewer can enter information that is later sent back to the owner of the Web site. You'll learn all about forms in Chapter Five, but for now, you'll just make a simple form that collects the user's name and a few other pieces of information.

To create a form you first set up *form delimiter*, an invisible rectangle into which you insert various *form objects* such as text fields and check boxes. To set up the form, place the text cursor at the point where the form will begin. Then choose Insert→Form from the menubar. This will create a wide, red-dotted rectangle on the page. Place the text cursor into this rectangle, and get ready to insert your form objects.

To collect the user's name, for instance, you'd type *Name:*, and then choose Insert→Form Objects→Text Field from the menubar. This will place a rectangular text field on the page. In the Properties window for this text field, assign it a name as shown in Figure 1.11. To collect other types of information, you can insert other types of form objects, such as Check Boxes, Radio Buttons, or Lists. Assign each one a name in the Properties window. And finally, at the bottom of the form delimiter, insert a Submit Button. Your form might look like Figure 1.11.

Figure 1.11 Web Page with Simple Form

When the viewer clicks the Submit Button in this form, where will the information go? This is called the *form action*, and it is set in the Properties window of the form delimiter. Click on the red edge of the form delimiter to see these properties. As you can see in Figure 1.12, the data in this form will be emailed to jlengel@bu.edu; when viewers click the button, their browsers will send an email to that address, the content of which will be the data that the viewers entered into the form.

Figure 1.12 Setting the Form Action

The email document that emanates from this form will arrive at the recipient (jlengel@bu.edu) in a form that looks like Figure 1.13.

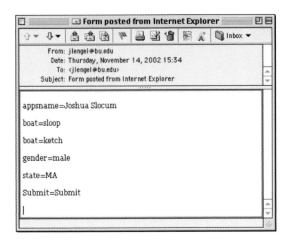

Figure 1.13 Email Received from Web Form

This brief introduction gets you started building a form with Dreamweaver. In Chapter Five, you will design and build your own form, step by step.

Add Rollover Images

Your sample site now contains all the things it needs to work: text, images, multimedia, forms, and links between the pages. You could stop right here and publish a useful Web site. But Dreamweaver makes it easy to add bells and whistles to your work—things you don't truly need to make the site work, but that might make it more attractive. As an example of this, you'll add some interactive images to your site—in this example, two images that display extra information when the viewer rolls over them with the mouse.

This topic is covered in more detail in Chapter Eight, and you may wish to save this aspect of your work until you reach this more complex addition in the last chapter.

For each rollover image, you need two pictures of exactly the same size, which will represent the before and after appearance of the image. You can create these pictures yourself in Photoshop or Fireworks (save them in JPEG or GIF format), or you can use the sample files provided with this chapter. In the *ch1sample* file on the Web Wizard site, these files are called *shoals1btn.gif* and *shoals2btn.gif* for the first image, and *apply1btn.gif* and *apply2btn.gif* for the second image.

When clicked, the first image will go to the page of the site that explains the shoals around Hog Island. These two images are shown in Figure 1.14. The image on the top is the original image that appears on the page when it opens in the browser. The image at the bottom is the rollover image that appears when the user rolls over the original image.

Figure 1.14 Images for Rollover Image

In Dreamweaver, place the text cursor where you want the rollover image to appear. Choose Insert→Interactive Images→Rollover Image from the menubar. Enter or browse to the two images for this button, as well as the page that the button will link to, as shown in Figure 1.15.

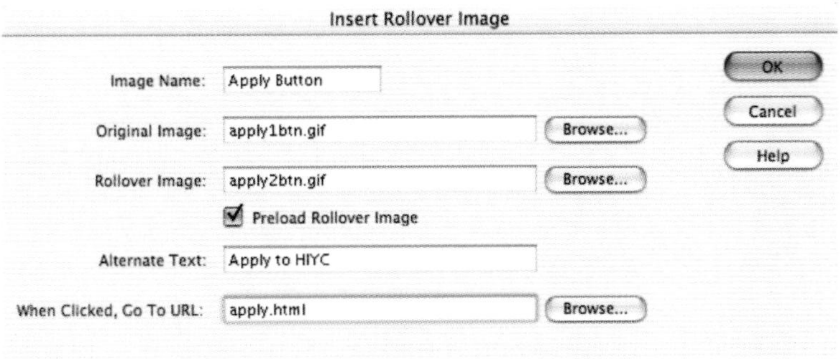

Insert Rollover Image

Image Name:	Apply Button
Original Image:	apply1btn.gif Browse...
Rollover Image:	apply2btn.gif Browse...
	☑ Preload Rollover Image
Alternate Text:	Apply to HIYC
When Clicked, Go To URL:	apply.html Browse...

OK
Cancel
Help

Figure 1.15 Creating a Rollover Button

Only the original image will appear in Dreamweaver. To see the rollover in action, you must preview in the browser.

You have completed your survey of Dreamweaver, worked with its basic functions, and built a small Web site. The rest of this book will expand on the details of working with Dreamweaver, taking you further on your voyage as a Web site developer.

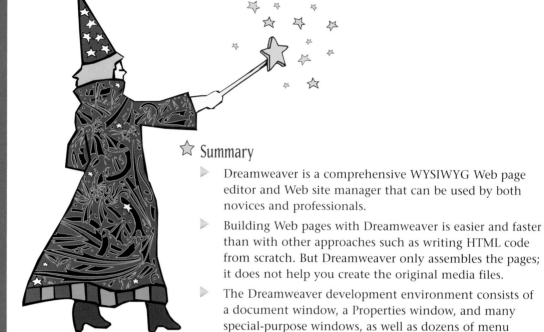

☆ Summary

▷ Dreamweaver is a comprehensive WYSIWYG Web page editor and Web site manager that can be used by both novices and professionals.

▷ Building Web pages with Dreamweaver is easier and faster than with other approaches such as writing HTML code from scratch. But Dreamweaver only assembles the pages; it does not help you create the original media files.

▷ The Dreamweaver development environment consists of a document window, a Properties window, and many special-purpose windows, as well as dozens of menu commands.

▷ It is easy to build a sample Web site with Dreamweaver that contains text, images, sound, video, animation, a form, and a rollover button.

☆ Online References

A video tutorial on getting started with Dreamweaver
`http://download.macromedia.com/pub/dreamweaver/tutorials/gettingstarted.mov`

A video tutorial on setting up the Dreamweaver development environment
`http://download.macromedia.com/pub/dreamweaver/tutorials/customizeworkspace.mov`

Printed tutorials on using Dreamweaver MX
`http://www.macromedia.com/support/dreamweaver/documentation/dwmx_tutorials.html`

Getting started with Dreamweaver, from the University of Wisconsin Eau Claire
`http://www.uwec.edu/help/DreamweaverMX/b-start.htm`

☆ Review Questions

1. List three aspects of Web site development that Dreamweaver can accomplish, and three that it cannot.

2. Explain the difference between creating a Web page with HTML and creating one with Dreamweaver.

3. List some of the media-preparation software tools that complement Dreamweaver.

4. Describe the two main windows of the Dreamweaver development environment, including the functions they perform.

5. Explain the steps required to place an image on a Web page with Dreamweaver.

6. Describe the process of inserting sound, video, or animation files into a Web page with Dreamweaver.

7. How do you make a hypertext link with Dreamweaver?

8. List the items necessary for creating a rollover image.

☆ Hands-On Exercises

1. Open a Web page in the browser, and then examine its source code (choose View→Source from the menubar). Estimate how many hours of study you think it would take you to be able to create such a page by writing the code directly.

2. Open Dreamweaver. Then open every one of its various windows, by using the Window menu. Examine each window. Then close the windows in turn until you are left with just the Editing and Properties windows.

3. Develop a Web page with various forms of text, using different fonts, sizes, alignments, colors, indentations, and styles. Save the page; then view it with Internet Explorer and then with Netscape. Make note of the differences in appearance between the browsers and the display in Dreamweaver's document window.

4. On the page you created in Exercise 3, insert an image. Align and position it in various ways in and around the text. Change its size. Save the page, and preview in both browsers. Note any differences in appearance.

5. Develop a simple Web site with text, images, sound, video, animation, links, a form, and rollover images. Preview it in both browsers.

WORKING WITH TEXT

 Raise the Mainsail

In many Web sites, the text carries the essence of the message. This chapter shows you how to prepare text for use in Dreamweaver, how to work with it in the Document window, how to edit and format it, and how to increase the chances that your text will be readable no matter what browser or platform your viewers are using. You'll also learn about how text works best on the Web, and how to get text from a word-processing file into Dreamweaver in the most efficient ways.

Think of the text as the mainsail of your Web voyager: It provides most of the power, it's at the center of the vessel, and it must be deployed properly to work effectively.

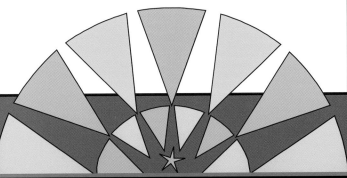

◎◎ Chapter Objectives

☆ To understand how text works in Dreamweaver, how Dreamweaver compares with a word processor, and how fonts work with browsers

☆ To learn the various ways of preparing text for Dreamweaver from existing files, from a word processor, and from other sources

☆ To find out how to insert or type text into Dreamweaver's Document window

☆ To learn how to arrange, edit, and format text on a Web page with Dreamweaver

☆ To learn how to arrange text items in a table or grid with Dreamweaver

☆ To be able to create a hypertext link from a word or phrase in the text of a Web page

◎◎ How Text Works in Dreamweaver

Just about every site on the Web contains text. Even the most graphic-intensive sites use text for navigation and explanation. This chapter deals with normal HTML text, the kind that is entered from the keyboard by the Web developer and displayed as standard text by the Web browser. Text that appears as part of a graphic logo, or as a stylized title for a page, is covered in Chapter Three; this kind of text is actually an image, and is treated as such by Dreamweaver.

The World Wide Web originated a system for the sharing of text files, and text is at the heart of HTML. Dreamweaver makes it simple to get text onto your Web page, and then edit and format it so that the viewer can read it easily.

Text in Dreamweaver

When Dreamweaver's Document window opens, it is waiting for you to enter text, with the text cursor blinking in the upper left corner. Text that you enter appears in the window as it will be seen in the browser. The text is in HTML code, without tags or formatting. But that's just the beginning of the story.

Dreamweaver provides an array of tools for working with text so that it will appear the way you want on the Web page. With these tools you may:

☆ change the size, style, font, or color of the text.

☆ align it left, right, or center.

☆ add headings or subheadings.

☆ link from a word in the text to another page on the Web.

☆ arrange the text in tables or columns.

The basic process for working with text in Dreamweaver is to first enter or import the text, then format and edit it, and finally check its quality.

Dreamweaver vs. Word

You can work with Dreamweaver as if it were a word processor like Microsoft Word. Simply enter your text and then edit it. If you are comfortable using the formatting toolbar in Microsoft Word, you will find that the Properties window in Dreamweaver provides many of the same functions, as shown in Figure 2.1.

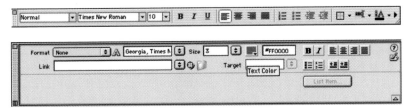

Figure 2.1 Word's Formatting Toolbar and Dreamweaver's Properties Window

If you are more comfortable using Word's menu items to modify the text, you will find that Dreamweaver provides a Text menu item that includes just about all the commands you might need to apply. The toolbars and menu items in both programs let you change font, style, size, color, indentation, and alignment of the text, as well as create bulleted or numbered lists.

However, you will also find some significant differences in working with text in Word and Dreamweaver:

* *Fonts*. Word lets you choose from a long list of fonts—whatever is available on your computer. Dreamweaver works with a limited set of font families that reflect what is available on most browsers.

* *Margins*. Dreamweaver provides no margin control and no ruler with tabs that you can slide to change the width of the column of text. Instead, you use Dreamweaver's Indent function.

* *Spelling*. Dreamweaver will not correct your spelling as you type, or highlight misspelled words for you. Instead, you must invoke the spell checker from the Text menu.

* *Tabs and Spaces*. Tabs don't work at all in Dreamweaver. Nor do repeated spaces. That's because these characters are not recognized by HTML browsers. To set up a list that lines up against a tab, use tables in Dreamweaver, as described in Chapter Six.

You can work with text in Dreamweaver pretty much as you can in Word, except for these few differences. If you are typing text from scratch, it's best to type it directly into Dreamweaver this way. Later in this chapter, you will learn how to import text from existing Word files into Dreamweaver.

☆**TIP**   **You Don't Need Microsoft Word**

Dreamweaver is fully capable of developing and editing text for a Web page. It includes all the tools you need to compose, style, and format the text of a Web page. Even though this book provides instructions for using Word, it's not a necessary option.

Fonts and Styles

Fonts and styles don't work on the Web the way they do in print. Most printers can handle any font in any size that you send them. But most Web browsers can only display a restricted number of fonts, in a few sizes; this is limited by the nature of the browser and the fonts installed on the viewer's computer. Thus Web developers cannot use any font they want, in any size, and expect all of their viewers to see it. Instead, they must anticipate the fonts likely to be installed on their viewers' computers and take into consideration the limitations of current browsers as they work with text in Dreamweaver.

Dreamweaver makes it easy to work within these limitations. Instead of listing every available font in the Text menus and Properties window, Dreamweaver lists a small set of font families as choices. These families are based on the fonts that most people have installed on their computers. And if viewers don't have the chosen font, Dreamweaver instructs their browser to use a substitute that's close in appearance to that font. For instance, if you set the body text of your Web page in Georgia, and the user does not have the Georgia font installed, his browser will display the text in Times New Roman, which is similar to Georgia. If the viewer lacks Times New Roman, he will see it in Times, and if he doesn't have Times, he will see it in whatever serif font the browser can find.

☆ **TIP**   Serifs

A serif font, such as Times or Georgia, includes little "feet" at the top and bottom of many of the letters, while a sans-serif font uses only plain strokes. The text in this tip is set in sans-serif font, while the regular paragraphs are set in a serif font.

Look at the list of font families in Dreamweaver by choosing Text→Font from the menubar. You will see five font families: two sans-serif (Arial and Verdana) and three serif (Times, Courier, and Georgia). When you select your text and choose a font family from the list, Dreamweaver generates the HTML code that manages the display on the user's browser. If you choose the Default setting, the text will appear in whatever font the user has set as the browser's default.

☆ **WARNING**   Keep It Simple

Even though Dreamweaver lets you format, style, and change the font and color of text, avoid the temptation to over-style the text of your Web page. Try not to use more than two font styles on a page, or three colors.

Text can be set in plain, bold, italic, or underline styles, or any combination of these. These are the styles that most browsers can display. Text can be aligned flush left, centered, or flush right, again because these are the alignments that the browsers can handle. And for size, your choices are limited to seven levels, with 1 being the smallest and 7 the largest, because this is how HTML handles text size.

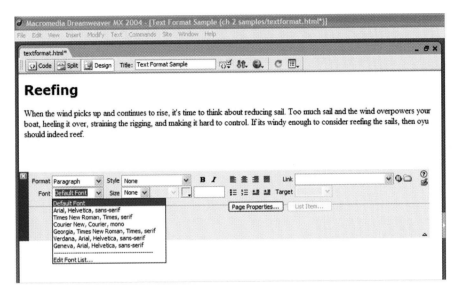

Figure 2.2 Formatting Text

When you set the text font, style, or size, Dreamweaver places a *tag* in the HTML code that tells the browser how to display the text. So if you format your text in Dreamweaver as in Figure 2.2, it will appear in HTML code as follows:

```
<p><font size="4" face="Verdana, Arial, Helvetica,
sans-serif"><strong>Reefing</strong></font></p>
<p><font size="3" face="Georgia, Times New Roman, Times,
serif">When the wind picks up and continues to rise, it's
time to think about <em>reefing,</em> or reducing sail. Too
much sail and the wind overpowers your boat, heeling it
over, straining the rigging, and making it hard to control.
If it's windy enough to consider reefing the sails, then
it's time to reef.</font></p>
```

The HTML code uses *tags* (set in red) and *attributes* (set in green) to tell the browser to display the text between the tags in a certain way. Notice that the tags use different terms than you might be used to from your word processor: what you call bold, HTML calls `<strong>`, and what you call italic is `<em>` (shorthand for *emphasis*).

Since HTML has no tags for outline text, 72-point type, or other nonstandard text styles, Dreamweaver will not let you set this kind of text.

Not all of your viewers will see the text of your Web page in exactly the same way. One might see the body text of the example in Figure 2.2 in the Georgia font, while it might appear in Times for another, depending on which fonts are installed on their computers. A viewer using Netscape or a Macintosh computer will see slightly smaller letters than an Explorer user or a Windows user, because of the different ways these two browsers and operating systems interpret the `size` attribute, as well as how the users have set their browser's font size preference. No matter how hard you try, you can't get Dreamweaver to ensure your Web page will display HTML text *identically* for every one of your viewers. Instead, let Dreamweaver create a page that will display text *acceptably* for all of your viewers.

The rest of this chapter will take you through the process of preparing text, getting it into Dreamweaver, and then formatting so that it is easily readable by the viewers of your Web site.

> ☆ **TIP**   **Planning and Organizing Your Site**
>
> If you are beginning the construction of your own sample site at this point, you might want to review the first part of Chapter Seven, which shows you how to set up a site folder and define your site with Dreamweaver.

◎◎ Preparing Text for Dreamweaver

Writing for the Web

Writing for the Web is not like writing for a magazine, newspaper, or business report. Because it is read from a computer display, often at a desk or on a lap in the midst of several other activities, text on a Web page should use a special style if it is to be effective. As a Web developer, at times you will be called on to compose your own words or prepare articles written elsewhere for use in Dreamweaver. Either way, keep these guidelines in mind:

☆ *Short.* Most people spend less time looking at a Web page than at a printed page, so you should write in short paragraphs with punchy sentences. Avoid long narrative exposition; use hyperlinks instead to send the reader off for these kinds of explanations. Write in short paragraphs that present information in digestible chunks.

☆ *Self-contained.* You never know how the reader will arrive at the page you are writing, so its text must contain enough information to set the context. You cannot assume that the reader has seen the previous page or has followed the path you designed to get to this page.

☆ *Straightforward.* Use regular words and phrases, as if you are speaking. Avoid unusual constructions such as his/her, never use the slash, avoid abbreviations, stay away from Latinate words such as *i.e.* and *etc.*, don't use ALL CAPS, and make sure every sentence uses an active verb.

☆ *Subheads.* Readers of Web pages often skim or scroll through text looking for the idea they are seeking—they seldom read every word. Use subheads to help them, more than you would use in printed text. A subhead every three or four paragraphs is a good idea.

☆ *Send-offs.* It's easy to refer to other sources, provide background information, and supply details with hypertext links. Embed links to other pages on your own site, or to other sites, to help the reader delve more deeply into the subject at hand.

☆ *Stylish.* The standard Web browser can display text in several different styles: plain paragraphs, bulleted lists, numbered lists, and definition lists. Consider using these list styles when you prepare your text. They are easy to format in Dreamweaver.

If the text comes to you as a Microsoft Word document, it's best to use Word to edit the document to fit these guidelines. If you're writing from scratch, it's best to write directly in the Dreamweaver document window. And if you are extracting text from other Web pages, there are some hints (covered below) that will make that easier.

Preparing Text in Microsoft Word

For many writers, Microsoft Word provides a comfortable and useful environment for composing text. It includes a set of familiar tools to make writing (and spelling) easier, and it's readily available to most people. And many of the documents that an organization wants to put onto a Web site exist already as Word files. A few tips will make it easier to use the text from Word in Dreamweaver:

☆ *Don't format the text.* Simply type your text in the default font, in normal style. Don't format the font style or paragraphs or the margins or the line spacing or the alignment. None of these will make their way through to Dreamweaver. Composing and editing can be done in Word, but formatting should be left to Dreamweaver.

☆ *Don't use tabs or repeated spaces.* These do not work on the Web, and will not be accepted by Dreamweaver.

☆ *Don't use tables.* Tables you create in Word cannot be copied and pasted into Dreamweaver. You'll create tables in Dreamweaver, into which you can paste the plain-text items from your Word document.

☆ *Don't insert pictures or diagrams.* These kinds of items will be inserted into Dreamweaver directly, separately from the text.

Once the text is composed in Word, check the spelling and grammar and save the document. Later you will copy and paste this text from Word into Dreamweaver.

Extracting Text from Existing Web Pages

Many Web-development projects consist of taking text from an organization's existing Web site and using it in a set of newly designed pages. You can do this by copying and pasting the text from a browser, or by saving the existing file to a file on the disk and then opening it with Dreamweaver.

Copy and Paste

This is the simplest and quickest method of getting text from an existing Web page into Dreamweaver, and it works best for short passages where the formatting need not be maintained.

1. Open the existing Web page in your Web browser.
2. Select the text you want to copy.
3. Choose Copy from the Edit menu.
4. Open the new page in Dreamweaver.
5. Choose Paste from the Edit menu.
6. Watch your text appear.

The words will appear in plain text, without any formatting. You will lose any font, style, size, or list formats from the existing page, but all of the text will come through. Since in many cases you will be setting the text in a different format from the old pages, this loss of formatting may not be a problem.

Save and Open

This method works best for longer passages and when you want to preserve the formatting of existing text.

1. Open the existing Web page in your Web browser.
2. Choose Save As from the File menu.
3. From the popup menu, choose HTML source as the format.
4. Assign a name to the file, and save it to your disk with an *.html* filename extension.
5. Open Dreamweaver.
6. Choose Open from the file menu.
7. Open the file that you just saved.
8. You will see the text appear in the Dreamweaver document window just as it appeared in the browser, with all the formatting intact.
9. If necessary, you can copy and paste this text into another Dreamweaver document.

You will notice that all parts of the existing page—images, formatting, titles, and other pieces—end up in the Dreamweaver document window. Just ignore these for now, and copy only the text you need.

Using an Editor

No matter which method you use to prepare your text, it's a good idea to have someone else read the words before you put them into your Web page. Most professional Web developers employ an editor who makes sure the Web site's writing is grammatical, easy to read, and in keeping with the organization's style guidelines. Even if you can't employ a professional editor, the suggestions from another person will in most cases lead to better text on your Web page. Send the text you are developing to the editor in a manner convenient for them—as a Word file, printed on paper, or in the body of an email. Ask your editor to return it to you with suggestions for style, grammar, and organization—and give a deadline.

It's a lot easier to make editorial changes to the text at this point in the development process than it is to wait until the pages are assembled in Dreamweaver.

◎◎ Inserting Text on a Web Page

Once it's prepared and edited, the text can be brought into Dreamweaver. You can type it in directly, paste it from another source, or import it from a Microsoft Word file.

Typing Text from the Keyboard

For short passages, or those where you are the author, typing directly from the keyboard into the Dreamweaver document window is the fastest and most efficient method. Simply type as you would with a word processor. Don't worry about formatting as you type—just get the words down. Separate paragraphs with a touch of the return key.

> ☆ **SHORTCUT** **Making Paragraphs in Dreamweaver**
>
> When you press Return while typing text into Dreamweaver, you get a new paragraph—Dreamweaver inserts the HTML </p> tag, indicating the end of a paragraph. This will show up in Dreamweaver and in the browser as a blank line between paragraphs. If you don't want this full paragraph break, but just a new line, then press Shift+Return on the keyboard. You'll get a new line, but not the blank line. In HTML, this is the
 or break tag.

Avoid the tab key. Don't use more than one space at a time. Remember that the function keys and keyboard shortcuts that you remember from Microsoft Word may not work in Dreamweaver. As you write, consider the guidelines for writing for the Web discussed earlier.

Some writers work better if they outline the contents of the entire page, and then go back and fill in the details. This can be done in Dreamweaver. Unlike Word, Dreamweaver does not check your spelling as you type. Later in this chapter you'll learn how to apply Dreamweaver's spell checker.

Pasting Text from Other Sources

If you want to use text from other sources in your Web page, you can simply copy and paste it from its source. You can copy from an existing Web page, from a Word document, or from any application that lets you select and copy text. Simply paste what you copy into the Dreamweaver document window.

☆ **WARNING** **Where's the Cursor?**

When you paste text into Dreamweaver, it will appear at the location of the text cursor—the blinking vertical line in the document window. Before you paste, make sure the cursor is blinking at the place where you want the text to appear.

The text will appear in Dreamweaver's default font, in the default size and color. Any formatting that was copied from the source will disappear when the text is pasted into Dreamweaver. Everything you paste will be in plain text, which you can later format using Dreamweaver's formatting tools.

When pasting from some sources, you will inadvertently copy other things beyond the text, such as images, special characters, carriage returns, and formatting devices that can make the text look strange in Dreamweaver. To get rid of these items, click the mouse just after them and then press *delete* or *backspace* from the keyboard. This removes the special character, and should set the text back to normal.

When pasting text from some documents, you may find that the carriage returns (the characters formed by the return key that causes a new line to start) appear at the end of each line and cause the text to appear uneven in Dreamweaver. The text can be fixed by deleting these returns. Dreamweaver's Find and Replace feature, described later in this chapter, makes this easy.

Text pasted from other sources still needs to be considered in terms of Web writing style, and should be spell-checked as described below.

Importing Text from Microsoft Word

You can copy and paste text from a Word document into Dreamweaver, but this loses all the formatting. However, it is possible to maintain the fonts, styles, and lists from an existing Word document. Here's how:

1. Open the document in Word.

2. From the File menu, choose Save As HTML or Save As Web page.

3. Assign a name to the file with the *.htm* or *.html* filename extension, and save it to your computer.

4. Open Dreamweaver.

5. From the File menu, choose Import→Word HTML.

6. In the Clean Up Word HTML dialog box that appears, check all the boxes and click OK.

7. See the text from the Word file appear in Dreamweaver.

Most of the formatting from Word should appear in Dreamweaver, from font to style to color. Some formatting may not work well on a Web page, so look it over carefully and edit it so that it looks good to you.

> ☆ **WARNING** **HTML from Word**
>
> When you save a document from Word in HTML format, Word uses some strange and unnecessary coding to format the text. This extra coding can make the text difficult to work with in Dreamweaver, and unpredictable in the browser. When you import HTML from Word, Dreamweaver automatically cleans it up, removing and replacing the Word HTML with more straightforward coding. For the most part, you do not see this process, since it happens within the program.

◎◎ Arranging and Formatting Text

Now that your text is in Dreamweaver, you need to arrange it so that it's easy for your viewers to read. Reading from a Web page on a computer screen is different from reading on paper, and this chapter explains how to use Dreamweaver to create text that's attractive and easy to read.

Fonts, Styles, and Sizes

As mentioned earlier, you can't use any font you desire on your Web page. It's best to choose from the list of commonly available fonts in the Dreamweaver font menu. The same concept applies to the size of the text—on the Web, text ranges in size from smallest (1) to largest (7), equivalent to 9 points and 48 points, respectively.

The body text of your Web page—the paragraphs of text that you expect the viewer to read as a narrative—should be set in a *serif* font, because that style is more *readable* for long passages. Serif fonts include Times, Georgia, and Courier and have little curls and feet on most of the letters. The text you are reading right now is in a serif font.

On the other hand, words set in *sans-serif* type are more *legible*—easier to read from a distance or in a quick glance. So, many designers use a sans-serif font for the heads and subheads of their Web pages. A sans-serif font, such as Helvetica, Arial, or Verdana, shows plain letters without feet or curls.

Figure 2.3 shows a Web page with the heads set in a sans-serif font and the body text in serif. Once you have chosen a set of fonts for your Web site, it's a good idea to use them consistently on all of the pages. These are not hard and fast rules about how to display text on a Web page. You can design an easy-to-read page in many different ways.

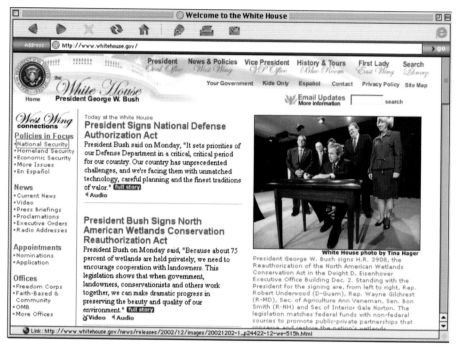

Figure 2.3 Web Page with Text

In Dreamweaver, you may set the font, style, and size using the Text menu items, or from the Properties window. As you learned in Chapter One, it's best to choose from the five font families listed in the Dreamweaver Text menu, from the seven sizes, and from the bold or italic styles. This will ensure acceptable appearance on most computers and most browsers. If you set no size, style, or font, the user's browser will display the text in its default, which for most people is 12-point Times.

Table 2.1 shows the possibilities for setting text size, font, and style in Dreamweaver.

Table 2.1 Font, Style, and Size Choices

Font Families

Default

Arial, Helvetica, sans-serif

Times New Roman, Times, serif

Courier New, Courier, mono

Georgia, Times New Roman, Times, serif

Verdana, Arial, Helvetica, sans-serif

(continues)

Table 2.1 Font, Style, and Size Choices (*continued*)

Font Styles
Plain
Bold
Italic
Underline

Font Sizes
Default
1 (tiny)
2 (small)
3 (normal size)
4 (large)
5 (larger)
6 (quite large)
7 (largest)

Table 2.2 shows when to use the various text styles.

Table 2.2 Style Guide

Style	Use It for...
Plain	Body text that the user will read as narrative. Plain style is easiest to read.
Bold	Heads, subheads, and words that need to stand out, such as glossary items.
Italic	Words to be emphasized, foreign words, and the titles of books and movies.
Underline	Avoid using this style.

☆WARNING Avoid Underlining

Underlined text is hard to read, and many users will expect underlined text to contain a hyperlink. It's best to set type as plain, bold, or italic, depending on its purpose.

To change any of these attributes of the text, select the text, then choose the desired font, style, or size from the Text menu. Don't mix too many fonts, styles, and sizes—this makes it hard to read. Stick with one size for headings and another for body text.

☆ **WARNING** **Browser Preferences**

No matter how you set the font and style of the text with Dreamweaver, your users may override these settings by changing the preferences on their browser. Both Netscape and Internet Explorer let the user override your settings for font and style, so your page may not appear exactly the same for all viewers.

Alignment and Line Width

In its default setting, Dreamweaver aligns text to the left margin, which for body text is the easiest to read. You can also align text to the center or to the right, which you may wish to use for titles, heads, and menu items, but should avoid for body text. A fourth choice, *justify*, aligns the text against both right and left margins, but to do so it must insert extra spaces between the words, which makes the text difficult to read. These alignment choices are shown in Figure 2.4.

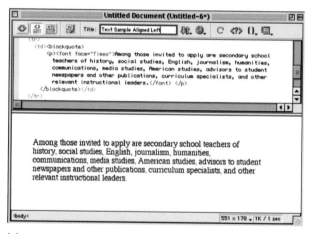

(a)

Figure 2.4 Four Choices of Text Alignment (*continued next page*)

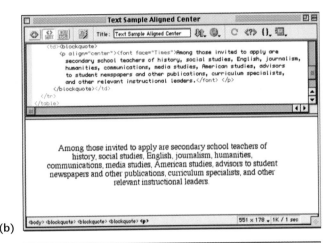

(b)

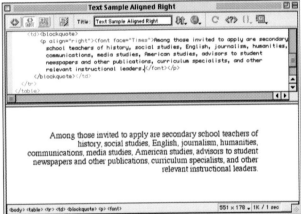

(c)

(d)

You can see in Figure 2.4 that the left-aligned body text is easiest to read. Notice also the width of the column of text. This paragraph is designed in Dreamweaver to be about 435 pixels wide, which results in about ten words per line; for most adults, this is the optimal line width for reading this kind of text. When there are more than ten words on a line, your eyes have trouble keeping track of which line to go to next. Narrower lines force your eyes into an unnatural vertical motion to read through a single sentence. Later in this chapter you will learn how to use tables to define the width of the text for ease of reading.

Heads and Subheads

The Web uses more *heads* and *subheads* than most paper publications. A head is the text at the top of a page or article, often in larger, bold type that tells what the page is about. A subhead is text within the page that indicates the title of a section. A very simple way to set a head or subhead in Dreamweaver is simply to isolate it from the rest of the text, and set its size and style appropriately from the Text menu. For most beginners building simple Web pages, this method will suffice. Set all your heads in a sans-serif font, bold, size 6; your subheads in the same font, bold, size 4; and leave the body text in default. This will display well and be easy to read and use.

Dreamweaver offers two additional methods that can make the setting of heads and subheads more efficient and consistent throughout your Web site: Heading Tags and Style Sheets.

Heading Tags

Isolate your head from the rest of the text and select it. Then choose Text→Paragraph Format→Heading 1 from the menubar, and see what happens. Dreamweaver set it in a large, bold style, and put some extra space above and below it. This text is encoded with the HTML <H1> tag, which tells the browser to display it as the largest heading style (in most browsers this is Times font in size 6). Heading 2 is a bit smaller, and the headings decrease in size down to Heading 6, which is smaller than the default body text. If you are consistent throughout your site, setting all heads as Heading 1 and all subheads as Heading 3, for instance, you have a fast and easy way of ensuring a consistent style.

☆ **SHORTCUT Use the Keyboard**

Using the heading tags can make the task of editing many pages of Web page text more efficient, especially if you use the keyboard shortcuts. Simply isolate and select the head, then press ⌘+1 (Macintosh) or Ctrl+1 (Windows) for a Heading 1. This is much faster than changing the font, size, and style with three separate mouseclicks.

Style Sheets

If you like the efficiency of using heading tags, but you want to better define what these headings will look like, Dreamweaver lets you set up a *style sheet* for your Web page (or for the entire site). With a style sheet, you define your own styles for heads, subheads, body text, captions, or other text elements that you plan to use more than once.

Suppose you wanted to make all your subheads Verdana bold, size 5, and dark red in color. Here's what you'd do:

1. Choose Text→CSS Styles→New CSS Style from the menubar.

2. Enter a name for this style, such as *subhead*.

3. Make sure the Make Custom Style or Class radio button is clicked, as shown in Figure 2.5, and click OK.

4. Assign a name for this style sheet, such as *mystylesheet*, and save it into your Web site folder.

5. In the CSS Style Definition dialog box, define the font, style, and color of this new subhead style, as shown in Figure 2.6.

6. Click OK when you have described the new style exactly as you want it.

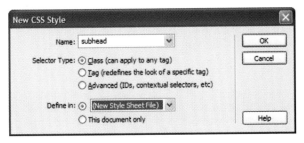

Figure 2.5 Creating a New CSS Style

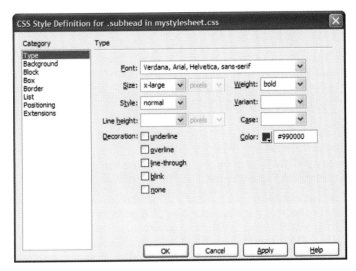

Figure 2.6 CSS Style Definition Box

This style will now show up in the CSS Styles menu. To apply this style to your text:

1. Select the text that you want to put into the new style.

2. Choose Text→CSS Styles→subhead (or whatever you named the new style).

3. Watch the text change to your new style.

☆**TIP**   **Cascading Style Sheets**

CSS stands for Cascading Style Sheets. The instructions above show you how to define a single new style in a style sheet. A style sheet can contain many different styles, one for subheads, one for body text, another for titles, and so on. A style sheet can even contain references to other style sheets. This cross-referencing of styles, one set of styles within another, is called *cascading*. For more information on this advanced topic, connect to *Best Practices with CSS in Dreamweaver MX* at `http://www.macromedia.com/desdev/mx/dreamweaver/articles/css_practices.html`

Style sheets can define more than just heads and subheads. They define all or most aspects of the page and help you to build a consistent site.

Paragraph Styles

A *paragraph* in Dreamweaver—the text that appears between two presses of the return key—can be formatted in several ways. As described above, the paragraph can be styled as a heading or with a CSS style. It can also be unformatted and so appear as normal body text. To do this, choose Text→Paragraph Format→None from the menubar.

A paragraph can also be indented, so that more space appears along its margins, as shown in Figure 2.7. To indent a paragraph, select it and then choose Text→Indent from the menubar. In HTML code, this indentation of the entire paragraph is called a *blockquote*.

In HTML, this kind of indented paragraph is tagged with `<blockquote>`, as you can see in Figure 2.7. Note that it's not just the first line of the paragraph that's indented, but all of the lines, so that the paragraph appears as a block. You can't indent part of a paragraph; the style you set applies to the entire paragraph.

Text and Images

Text and images are often mixed on a Web page, with the text seeming to wrap around the image. You'll learn about how to insert images and align them with the surrounding text in Chapter Three.

Sometimes what appears to be text on a Web page is really not HTML text at all, but an image of the text. Such an image is often used for stylized titles, menu items, and logos that require a particular font or unusual style that is beyond the capabilities of plain HTML text. Figure 2.8 shows some examples of text that appears as an image.

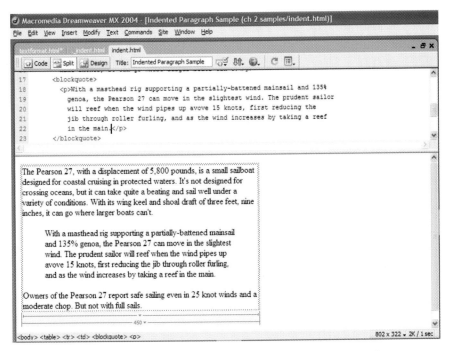

Figure 2.7 Indented Paragraph

Figure 2.8 Text as Image on the Dorling Kindersley Web Site

In Figure 2.8, some of the text you see is HTML text, and some is image text. Table 2.3 shows what's what.

Table 2.3 HTML Text and Image Text

HTML Text	Image Text
Inside dk.com in red at the left	dk.com at the upper left
Buy your loved ones presents...	Get it right this Christmas
Your shopping Basket, Your Account, Home . Help . Contact Us above menu items.	Menu items: Arts & Culture, Business...

You can't create image text in Dreamweaver. Instead, you must use a graphics program such as Fireworks or Photoshop to create the image, save the image as a file into your Web folder, and then insert it into a Dreamweaver document. This picture of the text is treated like any other image in Dreamweaver.

☆**TIP**   **Interactive Text**

You've seen menu text and other items on a Web page that animate or cascade when you roll over them. Dreamweaver can help you create these effects: They are called interactive images, including rollover images and Flash Text. These bells and whistles will be covered in Chapter Eight.

Columns on the Page

The Web site pictured in Figure 2.8 displays its text in three columns. To set up columns like this in Dreamweaver, you'd insert a table with three columns and one row. You'll get more complete instructions on using tables for page layout in Chapter Six, but for now, here's an easy way to set up a table for columns of text:

1. Choose Insert→Table from the menubar.
2. Enter the number of the number of rows (1), columns (3), the width of the table (600 pixels), the cell padding (5) and spacing (5) and the table border (0) in the Insert Table dialog box.
3. Click OK and watch the table appear on the page.
4. Enter or paste your text in the three columns of the table.

Figure 2.9 shows what this would look like in Dreamweaver.

Be careful when using multiple columns on a Web page—it's very easy to make the lines of text so narrow that they are difficult to read.

Arranging and Formatting Text

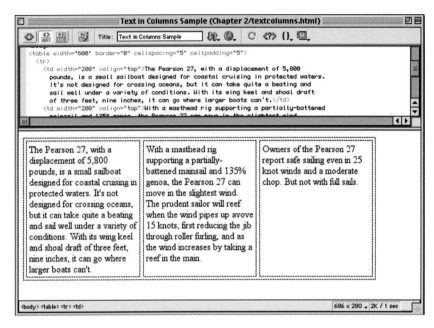

Figure 2.9 Text in Three Columns

Checking the Spelling

Even though you may have checked the spelling of the text in your word processor as you prepared it, check it again when your Web page is complete. Choose Text→Check Spelling from the menubar. Dreamweaver will check all of the HTML text on the page for proper spelling. There is no grammar checker, however, so you might want to send the page to an editor in addition to checking the spelling.

☆ **SHORTCUT   Multilingual Web Sites**

Working on a Web page in Finnish? French? Dutch? You can switch the spell checker to work on one of those languages and several others. To change the spelling dictionary, choose Edit→Preferences from the menubar, then select general in the categories list, then choose the language from the Dictionary tab at the lower right.

Finding and Replacing

Suppose you send your draft Web pages to the editor, who responds with the suggestion to change every instance of *U.S.* in the text of the Web site to *United States*. Dreamweaver can help you make this change, in two ways:

☆ If you are working on just one page, choose Edit→Find and Replace from the menubar. In the dialog box, make sure you search for text (not source code) in the current document (not the entire site). This is shown in Figure 2.10.

Arranging and Formatting Text

☆ To replace *U.S.* with *United States* on the entire site, choose Edit➔Find and Replace➔Entire Current Local Site from the menubar. This will look for all the files in your site—even if they are not open—and make the replacement.

Figure 2.10 Finding and Replacing Text

◎◎ Text Tables

Many Web pages display words and numbers together in a tabulated format, such as the page shown in Figure 2.11. In HTML, these numbers are handled as if they were text, so we will next discuss how to set up tabulations like this in Dreamweaver.

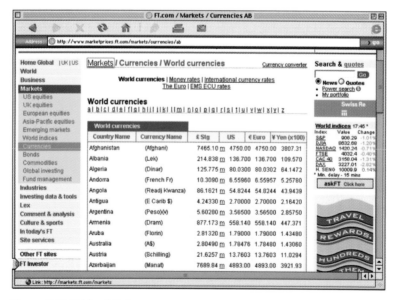

Figure 2.11 Table of Data

When to Use Tables

Whenever you want to display text or numbers in rows and columns, it's best to use a table. Tables are also useful in setting up a grid that can help to lay out items on a page, including images as well as text. Tables for general layout will be covered in Chapter Six, but here you will learn about tables of data such as what is shown in Figure 2.11.

On a word processor, you might use tabs or spaces to organize data into a table. But this won't work on the Web. A table is just about the only way to get the items to line up. And a table can give you easy control over the alignment, fonts, styles, and colors of the text in the table.

A table can appear as a grid, with many rows and columns, or as a simple block consisting of one row and one column, as shown in Figure 2.12. Each of the rectangles in a table is called a *cell*.

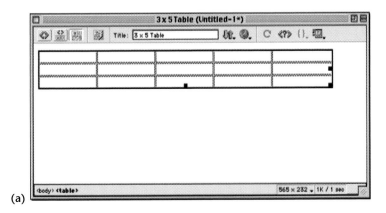

(a)

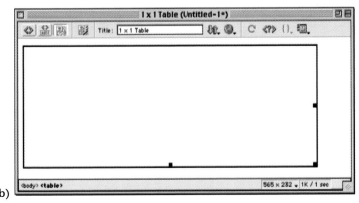

(b)

Figure 2.12 Two Kinds of Tables

A multi-celled table is sometimes used to lay out and align the elements of an entire Web page, or to present tabular data on a page. Single-celled tables are often used to make text appear in a line width that is appropriate for easy reading.

Inserting a Table

If you were to create a Web page on the schedule of tides at the Hog Island Yacht Club, you would organize the information into a multi-celled table. First, place the text cursor at the point where you want the table to appear. Then choose Insert→Table from the menubar. This will open a dialog box, as shown in Figure 2.13.

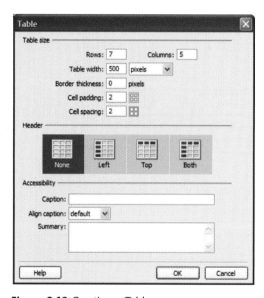

Figure 2.13 Creating a Table

This shows a table of 7 rows and 5 columns. When the table is inserted, it will contain blank cells. Enter the information in the cells, adjust the font, size, and style as necessary, and you have a table as shown in Figure 2.14.

☆ **SHORTCUT Adjusting Text in a Table**

It's easy to change all of the text in a table at once. Select the table by clicking on its outside edge (or by choosing Modify→Table→Select Table from the menubar). Then use the Text menu to change the font, size, style, or color of all of the text in the table.

When viewers see this page on the Web in their browser, they won't see the lines around the cells in the table. That's because the borders of the table were set to 0, as you saw in Figure 2.13.

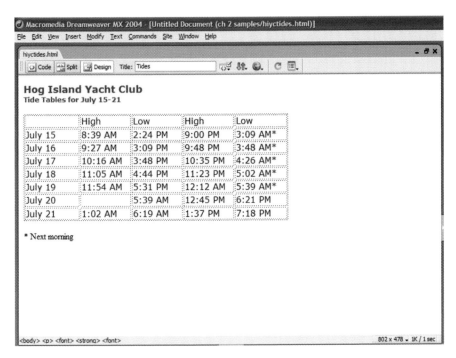

Figure 2.14 Text in a Table

Importing Tabular Data from Excel

Sometimes the information that you want to display in this kind of multi-celled table exists already in a spreadsheet such as Microsoft Excel. Dreamweaver makes it easy to insert tabular information from a spreadsheet. Here's how:

1. In Excel, choose Save As from the File menu.

2. Set the format to Text (Tab delimited).

3. Save the file (it will have a .txt filename extension) to your desktop.

4. In Dreamweaver, place the cursor where you want the table to appear.

5. Choose Insert→Table Objects→Import Tabular Data from the menubar.

6. Click the Browse button and find the file you just saved.

7. Click OK and the table will appear with the data from the spreadsheet.

   Once inserted, you can use all of the Dreamweaver text-formatting tools to change the appearance of the text in the table.

◉◎ Linking from Text

Any of the text on your Web page—a title, a table, or just a column of words—can become a link to another Web page. The linked text appears in blue, and when it is clicked, it takes the viewer to another page on your site or to anywhere else on the Web.

How Links Work

When you make a link from text, the words are tagged with HTML code that instructs the browser to go to the linked page whenever the text is clicked. Figure 2.15 shows what this looks like in Dreamweaver.

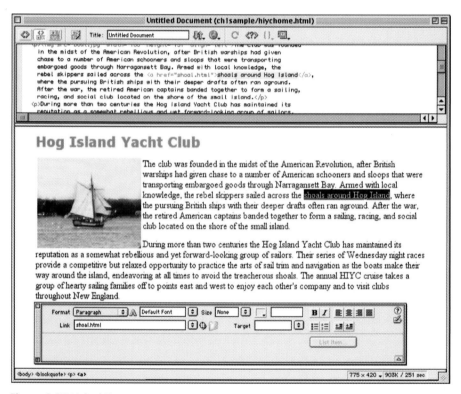

Figure 2.15 Linked Text

The HTML code for this link, which you can see in the code window, is `<a href="shoal.html">shoals around Hog Island</a>`. The text between the two anchor tags—*shoals around Hog Island*—shows blue in the browser, and the href attribute indicates the URL of the page to link to. Because this page is within the same site and in the same directory as the page you're coming from, the URL consists only of the filename. This is called a *relative* link. Had this link been to a site elsewhere on the Web, the link would need to be *absolute*, in a form such as `http://www.lengel.net/p27/`.

Making a Link from Text

To link from text in Dreamweaver, follow these steps:

1. Select the text you want to link from. You can select a single word, or a phrase of several words.
2. Choose Modify➔Make Link from the menubar.
3. Select or enter the name of the page you want to link to.
4. Click the Open button and the link will be inserted.

The linked text will appear in blue in the Dreamweaver document window. However, the link won't work in Dreamweaver. To test the link, you must preview the page in the browser, by choosing File➔Preview in Browser from the menubar.

Linking Within Your Site

In most cases, when you link to another page in your own Web site, you'll simply choose its filename from the list that appears in the Select File dialog box. You may find that the linking process works better if you save the page you're working on before you make any links from it. Make sure to save it into your Web site folder.

☆**WARNING** **Web Site Folder**

When you build a Web site, you need to plan the organization of the files that will make up the site. Set up a folder or folders that will contain all of the elements of the site—HTML pages as well as image and media files. *The Web Wizard's Guide to Web Design* can help you through this planning process. Chapter Seven of this Dreamweaver book can show you how to use the site management features of Dreamweaver to better organize your work.

In most cases, you will link to another Web page in your site by choosing one of the HTML files in the list. But you can also link from a word to an image, a sound, an animation, or a video. When the user clicks the link, the media file will be displayed in the browser window, taking the place of the Web page that you linked from. See "Setting the Link Target" below for more information on managing these media links.

Linking to Other Sites

Making a link from text to a Web page on another site is the same as linking within your site, except that you must type or paste the URL of the page into the Select File dialog box. The easiest and most accurate way to make an external link is to follow these steps:

1. In your Web browser, go to the page you want to link to.
2. Select its URL from the location box in the browser.
3. Copy the URL you've just selected (choose Edit➔Copy from the menubar).

4. In Dreamweaver, select the text that you want to link from.

5. Choose Modify→Make Link from the menubar.

6. Paste the URL of the link-to page into the URL field in the Select File dialog box.

7. Click the Open button and the link is made as the selected text turns blue.

8. To test the link, choose File→Preview in Browser from the menubar.

In most cases, these links will begin with http:// since they are absolute links, not within the file structure of your own site or server.

☆ **SHORTCUT** **Linking with the Properties Window**

There's a faster way to make links from text. You can select the text to link from, and then in the Properties Window, browse to or paste the link into the Link field.

Setting the Link Target

The links that you just created will open the linked page in the same browser window, replacing the page you linked from. In most cases, this is how you want it to work. But in some cases, especially when you link to a page on an external site, or when you link to a media file, you want it to open in its own browser window, leaving the original page open underneath it. To do this, you set the *target* of the link. The target is an attribute of the link.

To set the target of the link, select the link in the text. Then in the Properties Window, enter the target into the Target field. A target of *_blank* will open the page in a new browser window. Figure 2.16 shows how the target is set in the Properties window. Targets are also used to open pages in the various frames of a Web page, which will be covered in Chapter Six of this book.

Figure 2.16 Setting the Target for a Link

☆ Summary

▷ The process of working with text in Dreamweaver is similar but not identical to the process of working with text in a word processor such as Microsoft Word.

▷ The style of writing for the Web is different from other forms of publication, and may be prepared in a word processor or entered directly into Dreamweaver.

▷ Dreamweaver provides a variety of tools for formatting and arranging text for easy reading on the Web page.

▷ Tables are often used to arrange and align text in columns and rows, and to import tabular data from spreadsheets.

▷ Links can be made from a word or phrase in the text to a Web page in your own site or elsewhere on the Web.

☆ Online References

How users read on the Web, guides to help you prepare better text for Web pages
`http://www.useit.com/alertbox/9710a.html`

Writing for the Web, from Dartmouth College
`http://www.dartmouth.edu/~webteach/articles/text.html`

Writing for effective Web pages, from the University of St. Thomas
`http://www.iss.stthomas.edu/studyguides/writing_content.htm`

How to edit text with Dreamweaver, from the University of Washington
`http://catalyst.washington.edu/catalyst/how-to/dreamweaver/edit.html`

Basic text formatting with Dreamweaver, from Penn State
`http://ict.cas.psu.edu/training/instrmats/Dreamweaver/Text.html`

Text styles with Dreamweaver, from Macromedia
`http://www.macromedia.com/support/dreamweaver/layout/html_styles/html_styles03.html`

Cascading style sheets in Dreamweaver, from Macromedia
`http://www.macromedia.com/desdev/mx/dreamweaver/articles/css_practices.html`

☆ Review Questions

1. Describe a situation in which it would be best to prepare text for a Web page in Microsoft Word, and another situation in which it would be better to enter the text directly into Dreamweaver.

2. List at least three differences between Dreamweaver and Microsoft Word in their methods of text editing.

3. What are some things to remember when writing text for Web pages?

4. Explain the difference between HTML text and image text.

5. Explain some things you should consider in setting the font and style of the text in Dreamweaver.

6. Describe the steps involved in displaying text in a multi-celled table in Dreamweaver.

7. Explain how tabular data can be imported into Dreamweaver and arranged on the page for easy reading.

8. Describe the process of making a link from text to another Web page.

☆ Hands-On Exercises

1. Prepare a formatted text document in Microsoft Word, with varied fonts, styles, sizes, alignment, and indenting. Bring this text into Dreamweaver in at least three different ways (copy and paste, drag and drop, save and import as .txt, as .rtf, as HTML). Describe the differences in your results.

2. Develop text on a Web page that adheres to the style guidelines mentioned in this chapter, format it in Dreamweaver (including manipulation of font, style, size, alignment, heads, and subheads), and view it in a browser.

3. Prepare a table of text and numbers in Microsoft Excel. Bring it into Dreamweaver as a multi-celled table. Edit and reformat the table so that the data is as easy to read as possible. View the page in a browser.

4. Create and test links from text to another Web page on your site, to an external site, to an image, and to a media file. Open at least one of these links in a new window, using the target attribute.

5. Find a Web page in which the text is not easy to read. Save it to your hard disk as HTML source code. Then open it in Dreamweaver and reformat the text so that it is in keeping with good Web style and as easy to read as possible.

WORKING WITH IMAGES

 Raise
the Jib

Just as you could sail a sloop under mainsail alone, without the jib, you could also publish a Web page containing only text. But it won't go far in achieving your objectives. Images are a necessary and expected element of communication on the Web. This chapter shows you how to prepare images for use with Dreamweaver, how to insert them on the page, and how to use an image as a link to another Web page. You'll also learn how to make an image map with hot spots that lead to different places from the same picture. Like the jib on a sailboat, images can give your Web site the power it needs to reach its destination.

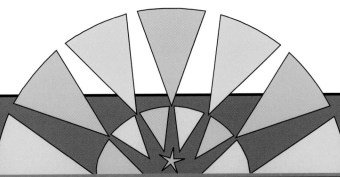

◎◎ Chapter Objectives

☆ To understand how images work in Dreamweaver

☆ To learn how to prepare and save images for use with Dreamweaver

☆ To be able to insert images onto a Web page with Dreamweaver

☆ To learn how to format and align images with Dreamweaver

☆ To understand how to make links from images to other Web resources

☆ To be able to create an image map with Dreamweaver

◎◎ How Images Work in Dreamweaver

A picture can be worth a thousand words. If you followed the instructions in the first two chapters of this book, you may indeed have built a Web site with hundreds of words. Now it's time to add some media to your site, with images. Images include photographs, maps, diagrams, charts, logos, and icons. It's unusual to find a Web site these days that does not include images. And it's difficult to think of a topic for which images would not assist in your communication with your audience.

But be careful—too many images can make a site confusing and make the pages slow to download. Use images only when they are necessary for good communication.

Dreamweaver provides an array of tools for working with images on a Web page, making it easy to include them in your site. But as you will see, the images need to be prepared carefully before you can insert them into a Dreamweaver document.

HTML, Images, and Browsers

The text of a Web page is included right inside the HTML code, but the images are not. Instead, the HTML code simply points the user's browser to the source of the image. Figure 3.1 shows a sample Web page containing both image and text.

If you look at the following excerpt of HTML from this page, you will clearly see the text—but you won't see the image.

```
<p><strong><font color="#EF1F1D" size="5" face="Verdana,
Arial, Helvetica, sans-serif">Hog Island Yacht
Club</font></strong></p>
<p><img src="boat.jpg" width="188" height="157"
align="left">
The club was founded in the midst of the American
Revolution, after British warships had given chase to a
number of American schooners and sloops that were trans-
porting embargoed goods through Narragansett Bay...
```

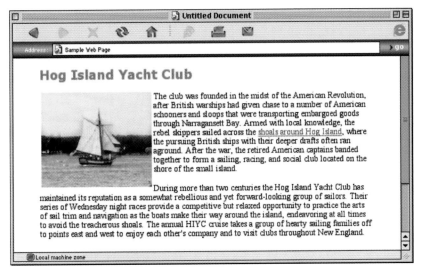

Figure 3.1 Sample Web Page

The information concerning the image is contained in the code indicated in red. It begins with an image tag img followed by attributes for the source of the image src, and then the width, height, and alignment of the image. This code instructs the browser to:

- display the headline text in a large bold red font,
- begin a new paragraph, and
- display the image file *boat.jpg* to the left of the rest of the text in the paragraph.

The browser follows these directions and shows the user the page that you see in Figure 3.1. The code provides the browser with a pointer to the *file* that contains the image, not the image itself.

☆ TIP   Find the Source

To understand how images work, open a Web page with your browser, then look at its HTML code by choosing View→Source from the menubar. Skim through the HTML code (or use Edit→Find from the menubar) and find the img tags. Notice the filenames of the images.

The important thing to remember is that the image file exists separately from the HTML file: It takes two different files to create the page in Figure 3.1. This means that the image file must be carefully prepared, and carefully saved, for it to work on the Web.

The ability to display images is built into all modern browsers—they don't need a plug-in to make images appear on the screen. But the browsers can only interpret certain kinds of image files; not all formats are supported. And the browser must be able to find the image that the HTML code points it to. If the image has been moved, or its name changes, the browser won't be able to find the image and it won't appear on the page.

Dreamweaver and Images

Dreamweaver lets you insert images onto a Web page, adjust them, and align them relative to the text on the page. You see the images in the Dreamweaver document window just as they will appear in the browser. And then Dreamweaver creates for you the HTML code that points to the image file. When you insert an image into a document, the image file remains outside of Dreamweaver. Dreamweaver remembers where the image file was located, and provides tools for managing the collection of image files that are included in your site.

Dreamweaver also lets you create links so that when viewers click on an image, or part of one, they will connect to another Web page. It also contains an advanced function that lets you create a Web photo album from a folder full of images.

Dreamweaver is not an image editor, however. It cannot darken, lighten, crop, draw, touch up, or combine images. For these functions, you need to use an image-editing program such as Photoshop to get the images ready before you work with them in Dreamweaver. Dreamweaver simply helps you to assemble existing images onto a Web page.

Steps in Working with Images

Much of the work with images happens before you open Dreamweaver. For images to succeed in their mission on a Web page, you must work through several steps:

☆ *Plan.* Every Web page needs a plan in advance of its assembly. While this book is not a manual of design (use *The Web Wizard's Guide to Web Design* if you need some planning help), you'll have more success with Dreamweaver if each of your pages has a plan. The plan for the page in Figure 3.1 began with a sketch like the one shown in Figure 3.2. This plan clearly shows the locations of the headline, the image, and the text of the Web page. It also notes the content, size, and filename of the image. The plan provides guidance for the preparation, insertion, and alignment of the image on the page. You can find more information on planning your site in Chapter Seven.

☆ *Prepare.* Few images are fully ready for appearance on a Web page. They might be the wrong size, the wrong shape, too light or too full of contrast, of less than optimal resolution, in the wrong file format, or improperly compressed. You must bring each image that you want to use into an image-editing program where you will prepare it according to your plan.

☆ *Insert.* Once prepared, use Dreamweaver to insert the image at the planned location on the Web page. It is at this point that Dreamweaver creates the HTML code that points to the image file.

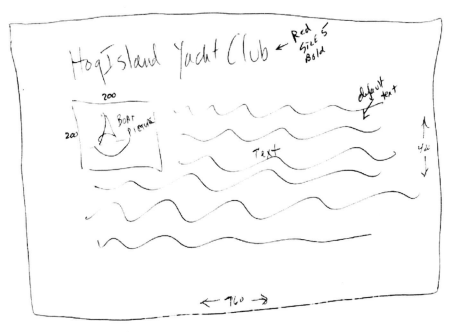

Figure 3.2 Sketch of Web Page

☆ *Align.* Move the image left, right, or center in relationship to the text on the page, or to the cell of the table into which you inserted it, according to your plan.

☆ *Link.* If called for in your plan, link this image to another Web page when the viewer clicks it.

☆ *Image map.* Some images contain more than one link. You can use Dreamweaver to create hot spots on the image that will lead viewers to various Web pages.

In most cases, you will prepare all of the images for a given Web page, build and test the entire page with Dreamweaver, and finally create any necessary links or image maps.

☆**TIP   Draw a Plan**

The best way to use this chapter is to build a simple Web page with images as you work through the steps. Begin by sketching a plan of your page that includes the content and location of the image, its size in pixels, and its filename.

◎◎ Preparing Images for Dreamweaver

There's a lot to consider when you prepare images for inclusion in a Dreamweaver document. You must first define exactly the nature of the image you need, as well as its purpose. Then you must plan where it will appear on the page and how big it will be. Armed with this definition, you can capture your image and then edit it with software such as Photoshop. When it's ready, save it in the appropriate format with a proper filename; as you do this, you'll compress the file.

Pictures on a Web Page: Why, What, and Where

Before you can begin preparing the images, you need to determine the kind of images your page needs. Does it need a simple illustration, as in Figure 3.1? Or a series of small thumbnail images as shown in Figure 3.3a? Or a large picture that takes up most of the page as shown in Figure 3.3b? Or a diagram? Or a logo? Or some small icons that link to other pages in the site?

Your first task is to spell out exactly the images you need, in terms of their:

☆ *Type*: Do you need a photo, a diagram, a logo, or an icon?

☆ *Content*: What will the image contain?

☆ *Size*: How big should it be, in pixels?

☆ *Location*: Exactly where on the page will it appear?

☆ *Filename*: What will the image file be named?

Table 3.1 shows a typical image specification table for a Web site.

Table 3.1 Image Specifications

Images	Type	Content	Size	Location	Filename
boat illustration	color photo	antique ship	188x157	upper left of home page	boat.jpg
HIYC logo	drawing	small pink hog	82x60	left of page headline	logopig.gif
6 boat thumbnails	color photos	members' boats	75x75	in table on boat list page	boat1t.jpg, boat2t.jpg, etc.
board of directors	color photo	board members group	400x275	center of BOD page	directors.jpg
docks diagram	diagram	dock layout	400x300	top of facilities page	docks.png

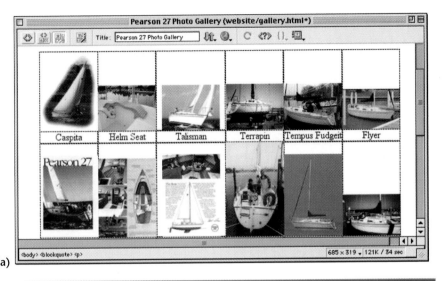

(a)

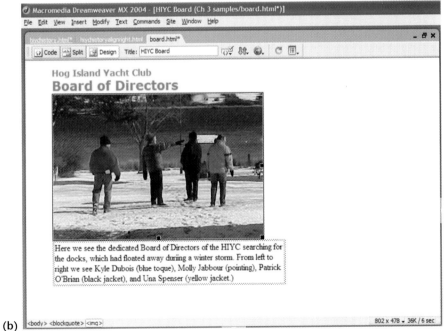

(b)

Figure 3.3 Types of Images

★ **WARNING** Plan Your Work, Work Your Plan

You will produce a better Web site if you plan your work before you open the program. Take the time before you begin work to specify your images as shown in Table 3.1. Otherwise you may find it difficult to manage and use your images in Dreamweaver.

Once the images are specified, you are ready to gather them. You can scan images from books or photos, shoot them with a digital camera, draw them with illustration software, copy them from an image collection on CD-ROM, or download them from the Web. For more detailed guidance on gathering images, see *The Web Wizard's Guide to Multimedia*.

★ **WARNING** Whose Image Is It?

Most images that you scan from a book or magazine or download from the Web belong to someone else. You should not publish them on a commercial Web site without permission from the owner. For more information on this topic, refer to *An Intellectual Property Law Primer for Multimedia and Web Developers*, by J. Dianne Brinson and Mark F. Radcliffe at `http://www.eff.org/CAF/law/ip-primer`.

Editing Images for Dreamweaver

Regardless of the source of your images, each one will need to be edited for content, style, size, and resolution before it is ready for use with Dreamweaver. Most Web developers use one of the image-editing programs in the Photoshop family for this work, but almost any image editor will do. For beginners, Adobe Photoshop Elements, a low-cost program that is often included with consumer-level digital cameras, is a good choice. It has all the tools you will need to prepare images for Dreamweaver. Other useful programs include Macromedia Fireworks, Paint Shop Pro, or Corel PhotoPaint.

★ **SHORTCUT** Use Sample Images

If you are unable to edit your own images, you may use the sample images posted on the Web Wizard companion site for this book at `http://www.aw-bc.com/webwizard`, and then proceed directly to Insert Images below.

You should go through a series of steps with each image:

1. *Set the color mode if necessary.* Photographic images should be in the *RGB* mode, where each color is represented in terms of how much Red, Green, and Blue is in each pixel. Drawings and logos can be in RGB or *Indexed* color mode. If you encounter an image in *CMYK* mode—a system designed for printing that represents colors as combinations of Cyan, Magenta, Yellow, and Black inks—you'll want to use the image-editing software to change it to RGB. In Photoshop Elements, choose Image➔Mode➔RGB from the menubar.

2. *Crop the image.* There are two reasons to crop images: to let the subject of the image fill the frame and to get the image into the shape called for in your specifications. Use the rectangular marquee tool in Photoshop Elements to select the desired part of the image, and then choose Image➔Crop from the menubar to crop it. Figure 3.4 shows the original photo of the board of directors of the Hog Island Yacht Club. The white frame shows the cropped portion of the photo that appears in Figure 3.3b. The cropped photo is better composed, and is the size called for in the specifications.

3. *Set the resolution.* Images for a Web page should be set to a resolution of 72 to 85 pixels per inch. That is the resolution of most computer displays. Setting a higher resolution will not cause the picture to display any better on the viewer's browser, and will only take longer to download. In Photoshop Elements, resolution is set with the Image➔Resize➔Image Size command from the menubar.

4. *Set the size.* Examine the size of your image in pixels, and compare it with the size called for in the specifications. In Photoshop Elements you can choose Image➔Resize➔Image Size to see the size and to set a new size. There's no problem making the image smaller than the original, but don't try to stretch it beyond about 120% of the original, or it will become blurry.

5. *Enhance the quality.* Perhaps the picture needs brightening, a distracting element removed, or a special effect added. Now is the time to use the adjustments and filters in your image-editing software to make the image look the way you want it to. *The Web Wizard's Guide to Multimedia* can help you with this step, as can the Photoshop support pages on the Adobe Web site at http://www.adobe.com.

Figure 3.4 Cropping a Photo

All types of images should be brought into the image-editing program and put through this sequence—including maps, drawings, and logos. As you will see in the next section, the only difference in preparation between photos and other types of images is the way that they are compressed and saved.

Saving Images for Dreamweaver

As you save the edited image, you will determine its file format, its compression, and its filename. These three are key to working with Dreamweaver—if you get them wrong, the images will not work properly on the Web.

☆ *File format.* Photographic images should be saved in the JPEG (.jpg) format. JPEG stands for Joint Photographer Experts Group, and represents a common method for compressing photo files. Line drawings, most maps, and most logos that contain lines and solid colors are best saved in the GIF (.gif) format. GIF stands for Graphics Interchange Format and works best for non-photographic images. If you are editing your images in Fireworks, you may find it easiest to save in the PNG (.png) format, which stands for Portable Network Graphics. Dreamweaver and today's browsers can work with all three formats.

☆ *Compression.* When you save the file, your image-editing program will provide some choices for how extensively you compress the image file. Lots of compression creates a smaller file that passes over the Web faster, but with noticeable loss of quality. Applying less compression results in more quality, but a larger file with longer download time. In most cases, choosing medium compression works best. As the ancient Greeks advised, moderation in all things is best, and today this includes image file compression.

☆ *Filename.* The Web demands certain types of filenames for images. If you use an improper filename, the images will not work with the browsers. Your images should be named simply and descriptively, using no spaces or characters other than numbers and letters. And the filename extension, such as .jpg or .gif, must match the file format. Also, it's best to use all lowercase letters, to avoid confusion with some Web servers. Table 3.2 shows some examples of improper filenames.

Proper filenames for the images in Table 3.2 would be *myboat.jpg*, *hiyclogo.gif*, *boarddirectors.jpg*, *docksdiagram.png*, and *clubhouse.jpg*. These filenames are acceptable in Dreamweaver, as well as with all browsers, and will be easy to work with as you build your site.

☆ **TIP**   **File Formats and Compression**

For a fuller explanation of image file formats and compression schemes, see *The Web Wizard's Guide to Multimedia*.

When you save your image from the image-editing program, use the Save As... or Save for Web command from the File menu. This will provide you with the opportunity to select the file type and to enter a proper filename.

☆ **SHORTCUT** **Save for Web**

With the newer versions of Photoshop, the best way to make sure your image file will work well with Dreamweaver is to choose Save for Web from the File menu. This will allow you to make all of the choices for file format and compression ratio in one window, as well as see their effects on image quality and download time.

Table 3.2 Improper Filenames

Type of File	File Format	Filename	Why It's Improper
photo of a boat	JPEG	my boat.gif	contains a space; filename extension does not match file format
HIYC logo	GIF	HIYC/logo.gif	contains a slash; uses uppercase letters
photo of board	JPEG	board.directors.jpg	contains two periods
diagram of docks	PNG	dia57342fgk67-85.png	non-descriptive filename
photo of clubhouse	Photoshop	clubhouse.psd	non-Web file format

Organizing Your Image Files

Don't just save your images in the most convenient folder. If you are building a small Web site with a dozen pages or less, you may set up a single folder, and save all of the files for your site into this folder. This will simplify your work with Dreamweaver. For a larger and more complex site, you should create a separate folder that will contain only the site's images. No matter which system you use, make sure that all your image files end up in this folder. (The folder itself should have a proper filename, with no filename extension. Many Web developers name the folder *images*.)

In Chapter Seven, you will learn how Dreamweaver can help you manage your site. But site management is dependent on your careful organization at the outset. If you haven't done so already, set up the folder or folders for your Web site, and use them as you work your way through this book.

◎⦿ Inserting Images on a Web Page

With your images properly prepared and organized, you are ready to insert them into a Dreamweaver document. To do this, you'll first set up the page to receive the image, insert it into the appropriate place, and then adjust it as necessary to achieve the desired effect. Along the way, you'll preview what the page will actually look like in the browser.

Set Up the Page

Before you can insert an image, you will need to set up a place for it in your Dreamweaver document. To set up a very simple page containing a title, an image, and some text, such as the HIYC Board of Directors page shown in Figure 3.3b, you would enter and format the title, then press ⌐Return⌐ to create a new paragraph. The picture will, in effect, be the new paragraph.

To set up a more complex page, such as the gallery of boats shown in Figure 3.3a, you would first insert a table in Dreamweaver, into which the images (and text) will be inserted. Chapter Six can help you format complex pages with tables or frames. For now, it may be easier to work with a simple page.

Whether simple or complex, the setup of your page needs to reflect the sketch you made in the planning process. Anything with more than two columns will require tables, but you can build a basic page with text and images, such as Figure 1.7, without first setting up a table. Set up the page, and then save it (with a proper filename) into your Web site folder.

☆**WARNING**   **Save to the Right Folder**

The Web page that will contain the image needs to be saved in your Web site folder, which in most cases is the folder that contains your images. Make sure when you save the Web page that it ends up there. If you save it elsewhere, Dreamweaver will have trouble finding the image files.

Insert the Image

To insert an image, place the cursor at the place where you want the image to appear. Then choose Insert→Image from the menubar. This will open the Select Image Source dialog box, as shown in Figure 3.5.

In most cases, you will use this dialog box to navigate to the folder that contains the images you prepared earlier; then select the image you need. Make sure the path to the image file is set Relative to Document in the popup menu at the bottom. Click Open, and the image will appear at the cursor location.

If your image does not appear in the Select Image Source dialog box, and you are sure it's there, then it has not been saved in a proper file format. Only JPEG, GIF, and PNG image files can be inserted into a Dreamweaver document, and their filenames must contain the correct extension.

☆ **SHORTCUT**   **Images from the Web**

You can easily insert an image from anywhere on the Web into the page you are building. Instead of selecting one of the files in your Web site folder in the dialog box shown in Figure 3.5, enter the URL of the image into the URL box.

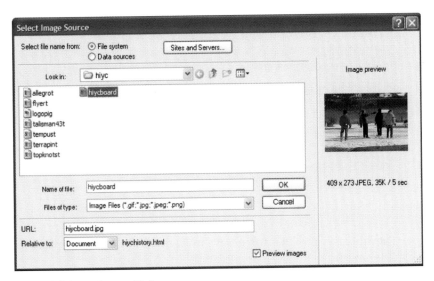

Figure 3.5 Insert Image Dialog

If your image was prepared in the correct size and format for the Web page you have planned, and if your page was set up properly, the image should appear in the Dreamweaver document window just as it will appear in the browser. If it appears as a small gray square with a broken image icon inside, then the image was not saved in a file format that Dreamweaver can read. The only way to fix the format is to open the image in Photoshop and re-save it in a proper format with a proper filename extension.

Preview the Page

Just to make sure, preview the page that you just built. Choose File→Preview in Browser→Internet Explorer (or Netscape) from the menubar. This will launch your favorite browser and then show the page in it. This is the best way to see exactly how your image will appear to the audience.

Adjust the Image

You may find that the image does not appear exactly as you had planned. You may need to adjust it.

☆ If it is too big or too small, too dark or too light, or the wrong shape, the best solution is to go back to Photoshop and edit it again.

☆ If is not lined up on the page as you desire, align the image by following the instructions in the next section.

Revise the Image

If the image needs editing after you have inserted it, there's not much that can be done in Dreamweaver. Your best bet is to undo the image insertion, go back to

Photoshop, and revise the image as necessary. The section of this chapter on Preparing Images for Dreamweaver can help you to edit it properly.

☆ **WARNING** Don't Stretch, Don't Shrink

Even though Dreamweaver can stretch or shrink an image to fit the space on a page, it's not a good idea to do this. It can pixelate the image, distort its content, and cause problems with some browsers. It's better if the images are displayed in their original size only.

After revising the image, save it back into your Web folder with the same filename, and insert it again.

◉◦ Aligning Images

Dreamweaver provides three ways to align an image on the page: text alignment tools, image alignment tool, or tables.

Left, Right, and Center

When you insert an image into Dreamweaver, it becomes part of the flow of the text—it's like another word in a sentence. In fact, if you insert an image in the middle of a sentence, it will stay there, and move back and forth with the other words as the sentence is edited. This is shown in Figure 3.6. Notice in the code window how the image appears between the words *logo* and *of*. However the text is aligned—left, right, or center—the image will also be aligned.

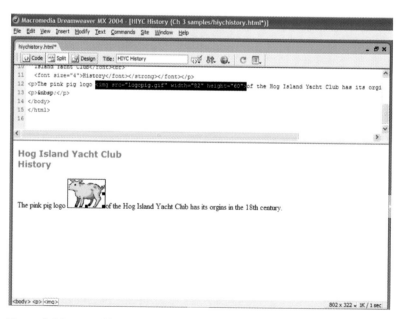

Figure 3.6 Image with Text

Figure 3.7 shows three versions of the same Web page, with the image on its own line, and the text aligned left (a), center (b), and right (c). Notice the alignment buttons in the Properties window, and the align tag in the code window. In this way, you can select the image and then use the text alignment buttons or the Text→Align menu items to position the image as if it were a word in the text.

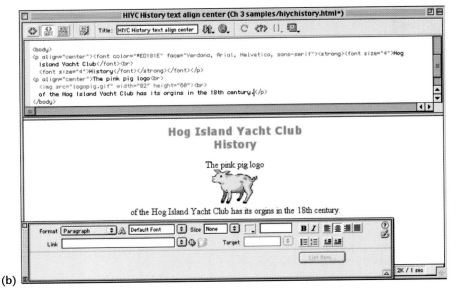

(a)

(b)

Figure 3.7 Image with Text (*continues*)

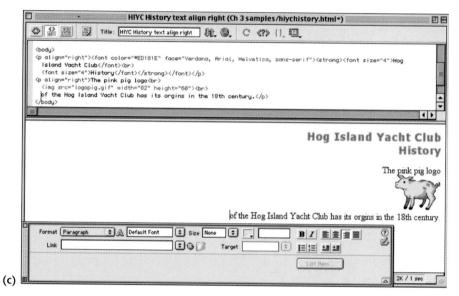

Figure 3.7 Image with Text (*continued*)

Align Next to Text

But what if you want the image to appear next to the text, as in Figure 3.8?

As you can see in the code window and in the Properties window, this is not an example of text alignment, but of image alignment—the alignment attribute is part of the img tag, and not of the text. The way to accomplish this is to:

1. Insert the image.
2. Select the image.
3. In the Properties window, choose Left from the Align popup menu on the lower right, as shown in Figure 3.9.
4. Watch the image align itself next to the text.

The text will flow around this image if it extends beyond the bottom of the image, as you can see in Figure 3.8. The image is embedded in the text as in a magazine or a book.

☆**WARNING Go with the Flow**

You can't control exactly how the text will flow around the image; this depends on how the viewer has set her browser, the display size of her fonts, and the nature of the browser and operating system. The text will always flow around the aligned image, but for some people the number of lines of text below the image may be a few more or less than others.

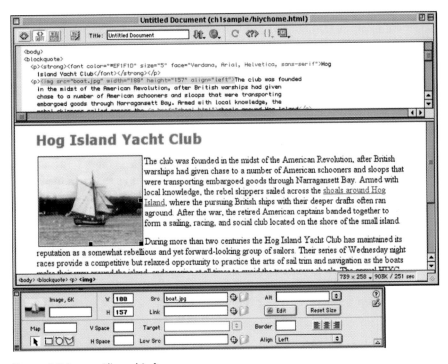

Figure 3.8 Image Aligned Left

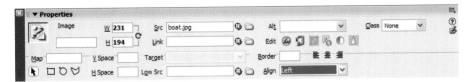

Figure 3.9 Image Alignment Dialog Box

Align in a Table

If you want the image to be independent of the text that's next to it, you can place it in a table. Think of the table as a grid that separates the Web page into columns and rows. The image goes in one column, and the text in another, as shown in Figure 3.10.

The entire page in Figure 3.10 is defined by a table that sets forth areas for masthead, columns of text, and pictures. Insert the table before the text or images are added to the page. Then place text and images into the various cells of the table. If you wanted to build a page with two columns, with the image in the left column, you'd follow these steps:

1. Choose Insert→Table from the menubar.

2. Into the Insert Table dialog box set up one row and two columns, with a border of 0.

3. See the table appear in the document window. (Don't worry; the table will get larger as you insert things into it.)

4. Place the cursor into the left cell of the table.

5. In the Properties window, set the cell's vertical alignment to Top, using the popup menu on the lower left. (If the alignment popup menu does not appear in your Properties window, expand the window by clicking the down arrow at the lower right.)

6. Choose Insert→Image from the file menu.

7. Find the image in your Web folder, and click Open.

8. See the image appear in the table. (If the image is wider than the cell, it will expand the cell to fit. You may need to drag the centerline of the table to the left to make the right cell wider.)

9. Enter the text of the page in the right cell of the table.

10. Enter other text (or images) as desired into the left cell under the image.

Figure 3.10 Image in a Table

The result will look like Figure 3.11 in Dreamweaver, and in the browser will look like Figure 3.12. Notice that the borders of the cells do not appear in the browser; that's because the border of this table was set to 0 when it was first created. Had you set the border to 1, it would have appeared in the browser as a line between the cells of the table.

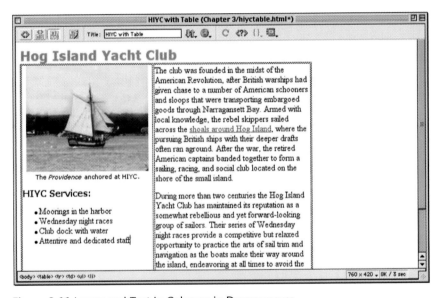

Figure 3.11 Image and Text in Columns in Dreamweaver

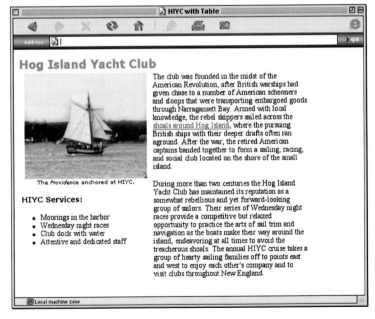

Figure 3.12 Image and Text in Columns in Browser

Tables are the safest and surest way to lay out a page in columns and rows so that images appear consistently aligned with the rest of the page.

Building a Thumbnail Gallery

Tables may also be used to display an array of *thumbnail images*—small pictures that when clicked open a larger version of the image on a new page. Thumbnail galleries are often used in catalogs, directories, and menus. To build a thumbnail gallery such as the one shown in Figure 3.14, follow these steps.

Prepare the Thumbnails

For best results, all of the thumbnails in your gallery should be the same size and shape. Use Photoshop to shrink and crop each image to a common size, such as 100 pixels wide and 75 pixels high. The actual size you choose depends on the number of thumbnails you plan to display and the space available for them on the page. Then use Save As from the File menu to save a copy with a new filename such as *pearson27t.jpg*, with the *t* indicating it's a thumbnail version of the larger photo.

Prepare the Link-to Pages

In most cases, each thumbnail will link to a different Web page. Prepare those pages now, inserting the larger version of the image and other information as necessary. It's a good idea to save these pages with filenames that match the filename of the image, such as *pearson27.html*.

Insert a Table

On the page that will contain the thumbnail gallery, choose Insert→Table from the menubar. Create enough rows and columns in the table to contain all of your thumbnails. Set the width of the table so that the pixel width divided by the number of columns equals the pixel width of your thumbnails. For example, if you have 16 thumbnails arranged in four rows and four columns, and each thumbnail is 100 pixels wide, and you want two pixels of space between the thumbnails, you'd set the width of the table to 4 times 102 or 408 pixels. And you'd set the Cell Space to 2. Both the Cell Pad (space around the image inside the cell) and the Border (line between the images) would be set to 0 (zero). Don't worry about the height of the table; that will set itself as you insert the thumbnails into the table. A sample Insert Table dialog box is shown in Figure 3.13.

Insert Thumbnail Images

Place the cursor in the top left cell of the table, and then choose Insert→Image from the menubar. Find the thumbnail image you want to show, and click Open. Watch the image display in the table. Insert the rest of the thumbnails, one in each cell, until the gallery is complete. Figure 3.14 shows the process of building such a gallery.

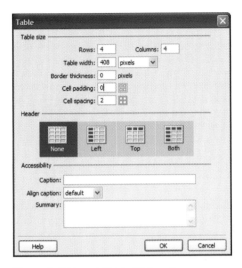

Figure 3.13 Insert Table Dialog Box

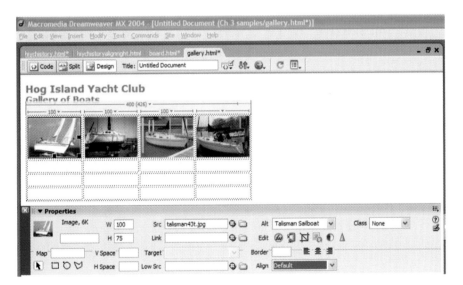

Figure 3.14 Building a Thumbnail Gallery

Make Links from Thumbnails

From each thumbnail image, you can make a link to another Web page—the page with the large image that you created earlier. Follow the instructions in the next section to make these links.

☆**TIP**　**Alt Tags**

Not everyone can see the images on your Web pages, whether they are thumbnails or landscapes. Visually impaired people, those who connect with very low bandwidth, and users of text-only devices may restrict their browsing to text alone. So if you use images for menus, they will not be able to navigate your site. However, you can add an *alt tag* for each image—a text alternative that will show in the text-only browser, or be spoken by the screen reader of the disabled viewer. To add an Alt tag to an image, select it, and then enter the text into the Alt Tag box in the Properties window. You can see the Alt tag in the Properties window in Figure 3.14.

◎◎ Linking from Images

An image can serve as a link to another Web resource: When the user clicks it, a new Web page is displayed. Making a link from an image is very much like making a link from text.

Link from an Entire Image

To link an image to another Web resource, follow these steps:

1. Select the image. You'll know it's selected when you can see the black handles in the corners.
2. Choose Modify→Make Link from the menubar.
3. Find the file you want to link to in the list, or enter the URL of the Web resource in the box.
4. Click Open.
5. The path to the link will show in the image's Properties window.

Don't try out this link in Dreamweaver—it won't work. To test the link you just made, choose File→Preview in Browser from the menubar, and see the page in your favorite browser. Click the link to test it.

Navigation Bars

Making a simple *navigation bar*—a row or column of buttons that serves as a common device throughout the Web site—is very much like making a thumbnail gallery with links. Follow these steps:

1. Create an image for each item in the navigation bar. All images should be the same size, and can be created easily with Photoshop or Fireworks. The images can contain words, pictures, or both. Use Save for Web so that each image will be in proper format.
2. Insert a table of the right size and shape to contain all of the images. A horizontal navigation bar needs a table of one row and as many columns as choices. A vertical bar needs one column and as many rows as choices. Set the cell spacing and padding and border as appropriate to your design.
3. Into each cell of the table insert the appropriate image.

4. Make a link from each image to the desired Web page in your site.

5. Include an explanatory Alt tag for each image.

6. Test the navigation bar in your Web browser.

Once created, this entire navigation bar table can be copied and pasted to other pages, and all of the images and links will carry over. This is a simple navigation bar, but in Chapter Eight you'll learn how to make a more complex and interactive navigation bar that changes as the user rolls the mouse over it.

◎◎ Building Image Maps

An image map is a set of several links from a single image. For instance, look back at Figure 3.3, the Web page that shows an image of the Board of Directors. With an image map, we could click on each member of the board in the picture, and link to his or her Web page. Dreamweaver makes it easy to create an image map.

Prepare the Image

To make a good image map, the picture must be large enough to enable the viewer to click on each item, and the items themselves should not overlap. The picture of the Board of Directors shown in Figure 3.3 is a good example. You should select the image carefully, and prepare it in the usual manner for a Web image, as described earlier in this chapter.

Create Link-to Pages

In this example, you'd make one Web page for each of the members of the Board of Directors, and save it to your Web folder. You can also link from an image map to pages on the Web outside your own site; in this case, you should find those pages and copy their URLs.

Insert the Image

Insert the image onto a Web page in the normal manner, following the directions given earlier in this chapter. In most cases, you will want to add a caption under the image that instructs users to click on the items they want to learn more about.

Create Hotspots

Select the image, and then look at its Properties window. In the lower left you will see the four hotspot tools: the pointer, the rectangle, the oval, and the polygon. (If the hotspot tools do not appear in your Properties window, expand the window by clicking the down arrow at the lower right.) You can see these tools in Figure 3.15. To create a hotspot, choose a tool, then click and drag it over the object you want to be clickable. When you let go, you'll see the hotspot, and the Properties window will change to allow you to make a link from the hot spot. To make a link to a page in your own site, click the file folder icon to the right of the link box. To make a link to another Web resource, paste its URL into the box. Include also an Alt tag for each hot spot.

A single picture can have many hotspots, each linking to a different Web page. Create the hotspots you need, link each one, and then preview in the browser.

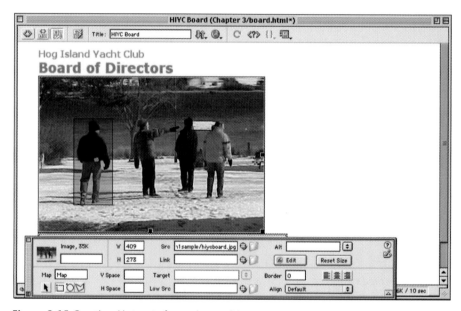

Figure 3.15 Creating Hotspots for an Image Map

Preview the Image Map

The only way to test an image map is to preview it in the browser. When the page opens, users will not see the hotspots, but they will notice the cursor change from an arrow to a hand as it rolls over the hotspot. A click on the hotspot will link to the target Web page; a click elsewhere in the picture accomplishes nothing.

Image maps can be used effectively with photos, diagrams, maps, and other types of images to provide simple and direct interactivity that makes a site easier to use.

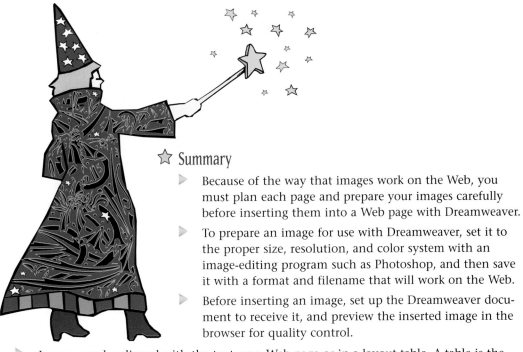

☆ Summary

▷ Because of the way that images work on the Web, you must plan each page and prepare your images carefully before inserting them into a Web page with Dreamweaver.

▷ To prepare an image for use with Dreamweaver, set it to the proper size, resolution, and color system with an image-editing program such as Photoshop, and then save it with a format and filename that will work on the Web.

▷ Before inserting an image, set up the Dreamweaver document to receive it, and preview the inserted image in the browser for quality control.

▷ Images can be aligned with the text on a Web page or in a layout table. A table is the best way to arrange images on a page.

▷ A link can be made from an image, or from part of an image, to another Web page.

▷ Navigation bars and image maps can be assembled from images, and are easy to build with Dreamweaver.

☆ Online References

Information about Adobe Photoshop Elements
`http://www.adobe.com/products/photoshopel/`

A review of image-editing programs from My Design Primer
`http://www.mydesignprimer.com/equipment/20008.html`

Information about JSC Paint Shop Pro
`http://www.jasc.com/products/psp/`

Information about Corel PhotoPaint
`http://www.corel.com/`

Information about Macromedia Fireworks
`http://www.macromedia.com/software/fireworks/`

Information about inserting and modifying images in Dreamweaver
`http://www.macromedia.com/support/dreamweaver/assets/insert_images/`

Tutorial on working with images in Dreamweaver
`http://tutorials.findtutorials.com/read/id/313`

☆ Review Questions

1. List the steps needed to work with images in Dreamweaver. Explain why each step is necessary.

2. What steps should be followed when preparing images for use with Dreamweaver?

3. How should images be saved so that they will work well with Dreamweaver?

4. Explain the process of inserting an image onto a Web page with Dreamweaver.

5. Describe at least two different ways of aligning images on a Web page with Dreamweaver.

6. How might thumbnail images be used on a Web page, and how are they built with Dreamweaver?

7. Explain the difference between a link from an image and an image map made with Dreamweaver.

8. Describe the process of constructing an image map with Dreamweaver.

☆ Hands-On Exercises

1. Examine a Web page from a popular commercial site. How many images are used on the page? Count the number of photos, logos, titles, and diagrams.

2. Develop an image specification table for a Web site that you are building, including type, content, size, location, and filename of each image.

3. Choose at least three images for your site and prepare them with an image-editing program. Adjust color mode, cropping, resolution, size, and quality as appropriate to your Web site. Save each in a format and with a filename that will work on the Web.

4. Insert these three images onto a Web page with Dreamweaver, aligning one with test alignment buttons, another with image alignment, and the third in a layout table.

5. Build another Web page that contains a thumbnail gallery of the three images that links to full-size images.

6. Choose one of your three images and build an image map that links to Web pages that explain the various items in the mapped image.

7. Use Dreamweaver to create a slide show from the three images you have been working with.

WORKING WITH MULTIMEDIA

Deploy the Spinnaker

O n a good day, with the wind at your back, you can hoist the spinnaker to achieve a faster ride. You don't *need* the big showy spinnaker to enjoy the sailing, but it sure makes it more fun. It's the same for multimedia on a Web site—seldom necessary, but under the right conditions, very effective. This chapter shows you how to use Dreamweaver to embed sound, animation, and video into a Web page. It also provides guidelines for the all-important task of preparing the multimedia files so that they will work well on the Web. Along the way, you will learn how you must take into consideration the bandwidth and browser capabilities of your audience, as you decide how much and what kind of multimedia to incorporate into your site.

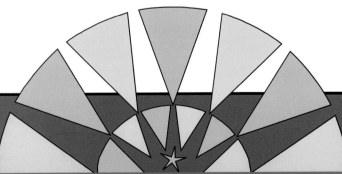

◎◎ Chapter Objectives

☆ To learn how multimedia works on the Web, and understand how it is built into a Dreamweaver document

☆ To understand how to prepare sound for inclusion in a Web page, import it into a Dreamweaver document, and provide for user control

☆ To be able to prepare animation for inclusion in a Web page and incorporate it into a Dreamweaver document

☆ To learn how to prepare video for inclusion in a Web page, import it into a Dreamweaver document, and provide for user control

☆ To understand how compression, file type, bandwidth, and plug-ins combine to set the limits on multimedia for your audience

◎◎ How Multimedia Works in Dreamweaver

Not every Web site needs sound, video, or animation; many of the most popular sites consist only of text and images. But when multimedia is needed, Dreamweaver enables you to include it easily.

Dreamweaver cannot create multimedia. It's not a sound capture device, a video editor, or an animation program. But it does provide tools for inserting multimedia elements into a Web page. Here's how it works.

Linked Files

Multimedia elements in a Web page are provided by sound, animation, or video files that are linked to the Web page. Just as the HTML code points to pictures with the `<img>` tag, the HTML code points to multimedia files with the EMBED or HREF tags. The multimedia information is not part of the Dreamweaver document; rather, the Dreamweaver document contains code that points to the multimedia file and tells the browser where and how to place it on the page. This means that before you sit down with Dreamweaver to create a page with multimedia, you must prepare each of the multimedia files you want to include.

☆ For voice or music, use a sound-editing program to capture, edit, and save the sound in a format that will work on the Web.

☆ For video, digitize the clip, edit it with video-editing software, and save it in a format that will work with most browsers.

☆ For animations, build the files outside of Dreamweaver with a program like Flash or Fireworks, and save them in Web-ready format.

You can then save these multimedia files—sometimes in the same folder as the rest of your Web site, and sometimes on a special server. Once saved, you can open Dreamweaver and insert the multimedia elements into the proper place on your Web page.

Figure 4.1 shows a Web page with a sound, a video, and an animation, as well as an image. This page requires five separate files on the Web site for its display:

1. The HTML page that includes the text, layout, and pointers to the multimedia files.

2. The JPEG .jpg file that contains the still picture of the old boat in the center left.

3. The Flash .swf file that contains the animated logo at the top right.

4. The QuickTime .mov file that contains the video of the boat race.

5. The QuickTime .mov file that contains the music to race by.

Figure 4.1 Sample Multimedia Web Page in the Browser

The same page in Dreamweaver looks like Figure 4.2. Notice that the multimedia elements display themselves as gray rectangles. While Dreamweaver can display images just as they appear in the browser, it does not contain within itself the power to play all of the different types of multimedia. So as you build multimedia pages, you will find yourself previewing often in the browser.

☆**WARNING** Don't Do This

Seldom should a single Web page contain this much multimedia. Such a page might confuse many viewers. The example shown in Figure 4.2 is intended to show how the various multimedia files work in Dreamweaver, not to illustrate good page design.

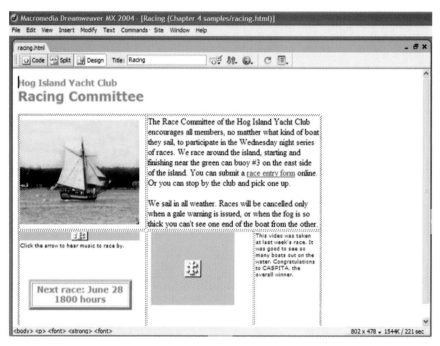

Figure 4.2 Sample Multimedia Web Page in Dreamweaver

The HTML code that Dreamweaver generates to embed these multimedia elements is quite complex. The code for the animation, for instance, looks like this:

```
<object classid="clsid:D27CDB6E-AE6D-11cf-96B8-444553540000"
codebase="http://download.macromedia.com/pub/shockwave/cabs/
flash/swflash.cab#version=6,0,29,0" width="317" height="41">
        <param name="movie" value="hiyclogo.swf">
        <param name="quality" value="high">
        <embed src="hiyclogo.swf" quality="high"
pluginspage="http://www.macromedia.com/go/getflashplayer"
type="application/x-shockwave-flash" width="317"
height="41"></embed></object>
```

That's quite a lot of code for a single item on a Web page! We need so much code for multimedia because:

⭐ the ability to display sound, video, and animation is not built into the common browsers.

⭐ multimedia items come in many different file types and formats, each of which needs its own *plug-in*, an addition to the browser that allows the media to play.

⭐ multimedia elements often include extra parameters that set size, quality, and user control.

The key item in this code that actually points to the multimedia file and places it on the page is shown in red in the sample above: embed src="hiyclogo.swf". The embed tag tells the browser to embed the multimedia object onto the page at this point in the text, and points it to the source of the file. The rest of the code tells the browser how to find the plug-in it needs to display the multimedia item, and what parameters to use in displaying it.

File Types and Plug-ins

In this book we cannot cover all of the multimedia file types that are used on the Web, or explain how the plug-ins work. *The Web Wizard's Guide to Multimedia* discusses those topics in more detail. Dreamweaver recognizes and can insert into your Web pages all of the commonly used multimedia file types, and many not-so-common file types. And it also knows about plug-ins, and automatically generates the information the browser needs to make the plug-ins work. But it cannot "read" the multimedia files you give to it, nor can it guarantee they are in the right format, or that they will work in your audience's browser.

In each section of this chapter, you will learn about the most commonly used file formats and plug-ins for sound, video, and animation on the Web, as listed in Table 4.1.

Table 4.1 Multimedia File Types

Media Type	File Type	Filename Extension	Plug-in
Sound	AIFF	.aif	QuickTime, Windows Media, RealPlayer
	QuickTime	.mov	QuickTime
	MP3	.mp3	QuickTime, Windows Media, RealPlayer
	WAVE	.wav	QuickTime, Windows Media, RealPlayer
	Real Audio	.ram, .ra, .rm	Real Player
	Flash	.swf, .swa	Flash Player
Animation	Flash	.swf	Flash Player
	Shockwave	.dcr	Shockwave Player
	Animated GIF or PNG	.gif, .png	Not needed
Video	QuickTime	.mov	QuickTime
	RealPlayer	.ra, .ram, .rm	Real Player
	Windows Media	.asf	Windows Media
	MPEG	.mpg	QuickTime
	Flash	.swf	Flash Player

All of these types, plus others such as Java Applets and ActiveX controls, can be embedded into a Web page with Dreamweaver. And the methods for inserting each type are quite similar. It's easy to insert the multimedia on the page with Dreamweaver; what is difficult is preparing the media files properly so that they work with the audience's browsers.

Bandwidth

Not everyone can play multimedia on their computer. People without speakers can't hear the sound, and those with older computers don't have the processing power to display video. Many lack the latest plug-ins for animation, or for the newest varieties of video files. But the largest source of disappointment with multimedia on the Web stems from lack of bandwidth.

Multimedia files (especially video files) are large, even after they have been compressed. To move these files across the Internet from the server to the audience's computer causes millions of bits and bytes to flow through the network. Without a connection that can pass thousands of bits every second, the files will not arrive in a timely fashion, and the user will not enjoy a good multimedia experience. And time is the key here: Sound, video and animation all occur over a definite span of time, so if the data arrive too late, viewers and listeners will not see or hear it properly. You can find more information about the limitations of bandwidth and about how media files are compressed to take less time to travel in *The Web Wizard's Guide to Multimedia.*

When putting multimedia files into your Dreamweaver documents, you must plan in advance to make sure that your audience will actually be able to receive them and display them in a useful way. As you cover each type of media in this chapter, you will learn some rules of thumb for the amount of multimedia that you can expect your users to handle. Table 4.2 shows the kinds of multimedia that work well at various bandwidths.

Table 4.2 Multimedia Possibilities at Various Bandwidths

Connection	Bandwidth	Multimedia Possibilities
56K modem	56 kilobits per second	Images, animation, compressed audio, very small highly compressed video
ISDN (Integrated Service Digital Network)	128 kilobits per second	Images, animation, compressed audio, small highly compressed video
DSL (Digital Subscriber Line)	512 kilobits per second (at best)	Images, animation, compressed audio, medium highly compressed video (at best)
Cable Modem	512 kilobits per second	Images, animation, compressed audio, medium highly compressed video
T1 line	1.5 megabits per second	Images, animation, high-quality compressed audio, large highly compressed video
Ethernet	10 or 100 megabits per second	Images, animation, high-quality audio, large compressed video

◎◎ Working with Sound

Sound on a Web page created with Dreamweaver can come in many forms—a piece of music that plays in the background, a spoken explanation of a complex diagram, or a special effect to accompany a visual event. Sound can play automatically, or be clicked and controlled by the user. A Web page can reference an archive of recorded sounds, or play a live stream in real time. If you are working on your own Web site as you read this book, think of the many ways that sound can be used to help communicate your message.

☆**WARNING** Don't Annoy

Sounds that play over and over on a Web page, or video clips that can't be controlled by the viewer can annoy the audience. Use these media only when necessary, and give the user the power to turn them off.

Dreamweaver cannot record sound, edit it, or save it in the proper format. Dreamweaver does help you insert into a Web page sound that you have already prepared and saved. It also helps you control the way that the sound appears, and the amount of control the user has over it.

Preparing Sound

Most Web developers use a sound-editing program to record, edit, and save sounds in formats suitable to both the Web and their audience. The selection and use of sound-editing programs is beyond the scope of this book. Choose an editor that can compress and save sounds in the formats appropriate to your audience.

☆ **SHORTCUT** Use the Sample Files

Not enough time to prepare your own multimedia files? Missing the editing programs? Then use the sample files provided on the *Web Wizard* companion site for this book. These are the same files mentioned in the sample site, and may be downloaded onto your computer.

If it's music you need, then the .mp3 format is probably the best for most users. It has become the most popular format for music on the Web, and most audiences are equipped to receive and play .mp3 files with their browsers. MP3 files can be played by the QuickTime, RealPlayer, and Windows Media plug-ins. But avoid putting entire tracks from a CD on your Web page because they are too big for easy reception by most users, and are almost always copyrighted material. It is better to use an excerpt, and to record your own music. Other good formats for music include QuickTime (.mov), MIDI (.mid), and Windows Media Audio (.wma). These can be compressed to small file sizes, work on all platforms, and do not require a proprietary Web server.

If you are using voice or sound effects on your Web page, you can save it in the QuickTime (.mov) or Flash (.swf or .swa) formats. These provide good compression and good quality; they also work on all platforms and don't need a special server.

As you compress and save your sound from the editor, you will have to make choices about the type and amount of compression to apply. The more you compress the data, the faster it will arrive at your user's browser—but the lower its quality will be. You should conduct some trial-and-error testing to find the best compression for your needs. *The Web Wizard's Guide to Multimedia* can provide more help on editing and compressing sound files.

While other sound formats can be used both on the Web and with Dreamweaver, such as .wav, .aif, and .au, these are uncompressed formats that in most cases have been superseded by the newer and more efficient formats.

And unless your organization has licensed and installed a RealNetworks media server—required for the RealPlayer streaming formats—you should choose one of the formats that does not require a special server.

After you have prepared your sound files, check their file sizes against the capabilities of your audience. If your audience consists of computer engineers with powerful computers on fiber-optic connections, you can use larger files. But if your audience includes a good number of folks with dial-up modem connections, you must keep the size of your sound files small. Table 4.3 shows about how long it will take users to download files of various sizes. As you can see, for all but the highest-bandwidth users, sound files much larger than a megabyte in size will take too long to arrive to be useful. So think twice, and check the file size carefully, before you take your sound to Dreamweaver.

Table 4.3 Download Times for Various File Sizes on Various Connections

Connection	250 Kilobytes	3 Megabytes	10 Megabytes
56K modem	2 minutes	30 minutes	1.5 hours
Cable modem or DSL	15 seconds	5 minutes	15 minutes
T1 line	7 seconds	2 minutes	7 minutes
Ethernet or LAN direct	1 second	10 seconds	1 minute

Streaming Audio

So far this discussion of sound on the Web has assumed that the entire sound file is being downloaded to the user and played when it is complete. But Dreamweaver can also include various forms of *streaming audio* (and video as well) in a Web page. One type of streaming is called *progressive download*, and the other is *real-time streaming*.

Progressive Download

With a progressive download, the file begins to download to the user, and after some of the data has arrived, the file begins playing. As it plays, the rest of the file continues to load. Progressive download is most often used with Flash (.swf) or QuickTime (.mov) audio (and video) files. It can work well in situations where the *data rate* of the file—the number of bits of data that it plays each second—is lower than the data rate of the user's connection. So for a user on a 56K modem connection, progressive download will work as long as the data rate of the file is less than 56K.

Real-time Streaming

In this method, the sound file never downloads to your audience's computer. Instead, a special streaming media server sends the file in a stream of data to the members of the audience, and their computers play the sound as soon as it arrives. Again, the data rate of the streaming file must be less than the data rate of the user's connection for this method to work. RealAudio and the Internet radio stations that you find with iTunes use this kind of streaming. Real-time streaming allows very long sound files that would be much too large for downloading to be played continuously on a Web page. It also keeps files from being copied, since that data is never saved to the user's hard drive.

If your organization has access to a streaming server, and if your site needs lots of voice and music over a long period, then streaming is the way to go.

Data Rate

For both kinds of streaming, the data rate of the sound file is critical to the user's experience. As a sound file plays back to the user, it sends a certain number of bits of data through the system, which are converted to audible sound by the computer and the speakers (or headphones). The higher the sound quality, the higher the data rate. An uncompressed track from a music CD, for instance, will have a data rate of 704 kilobits per second—much too much data to stream through all but the fastest connections. The same song compressed with MP3 would have a data rate of about 20 kilobits per second, much more amenable to streaming.

You can learn the data rate of a sound file by opening it with a program such as QuickTime Player Pro, and then choosing Get Movie Properties from the Movie menu. This opens a panel where you can see the data rate and other information about the file. This is shown in Figure 4.3.

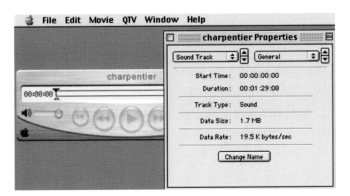

Figure 4.3 Examining the Data Rate of a Sound File

A good rule of thumb is to compress your streaming sound file so that its data rate is lower than the connection speed of the bulk of your audience.

Saving the Sound File

As you save your sound file, you need to consider its file format, compression, and filename. The file format should be chosen to fit the type of sound needed as well as the capabilities of your users, as described above. In most cases, you will save music in .mp3 or .mov, voice in QuickTime (.mov) format. Table 4.4 shows some typical parameters for saving sound files that will not be streamed.

Table 4.4 Typical Parameters for Saving Downloaded Sound Files

Type of Sound	File Format	Compression	Filename Extension
Music	MP3	MP3	.mp3
	Windows Media	Windows Media	.wma of .asf
	QuickTime	MP3 or QdesignMusic	.mov
Voice	QuickTime	Qualcomm Purevoice	.mov
	Windows Media	Windows Media	.wma of .asf
	Flash (also called Shockwave audio)	Flash Sound Codec	.swf or .swa

If you have access to a streaming server, you might also use one of the RealAudio formats or the QuickTime hinted streaming format. In this case, you should save the file in the special streaming format using RealProducer or QuickTime player Pro, or other sound-editing program. When you save, you get to choose the data rate of the file, which must be matched to the connection speed of your typical user.

Where to Save

Short sound files that will be downloaded to the user, including those saved in the progressive download format, should be carefully saved to the appropriate folder of your Web site. Many Web developers who have a large number of sound files in their site set up a *sounds* folder within their Web site folder, and save all sounds in it. Others save sound, video, and animation into a *media* folder. If your site is small, with a manageable number of files, you can save the sound files in the same folder as your HTML and image files.

However, if you use true streaming, you must save your files to a special folder on the streaming server, which your webmaster will identify for you. With RealAudio, the webmaster will provide you with a *pathname* to the file on the streaming server. With QuickTime streaming, you will make a *reference file* that serves as an alias to the stream; you will save this reference file to your Web folder.

No matter where you save, be sure to use a filename that will work on the Web, and a filename extension that matches the file format.

Once your sound is saved in the proper format in the right place with an appropriate filename, you are ready to insert it into a Dreamweaver document.

Inserting Sound

Sound on a Web page can be *embedded* or *linked*. Embedded sound appears (plays) right on the page. Linked sound plays in a separate browser or player window. Dreamweaver can help you include both kinds of sound. It can also provide a third method, called the Play Sound Behavior, that uses Javascript to play a sound file when a user clicks an object.

Embedded Sound

To embed a sound in a Web page, choose Insert→Media→Plugin from Dreamweaver's menubar. Then use the dialog box to navigate to the sound file you need, as shown in Figure 4.4.

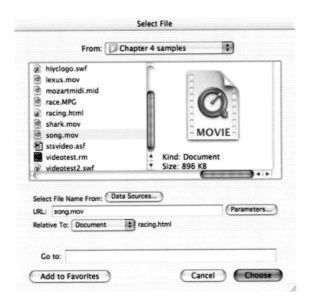

Figure 4.4 Inserting an Embedded Sound

By examining the filename extension of the file, Dreamweaver will include the HTML code for the appropriate plug-in player for the file format of the sound. And it will show the sound in the document window as a gray square, as shown in Figure 4.5.

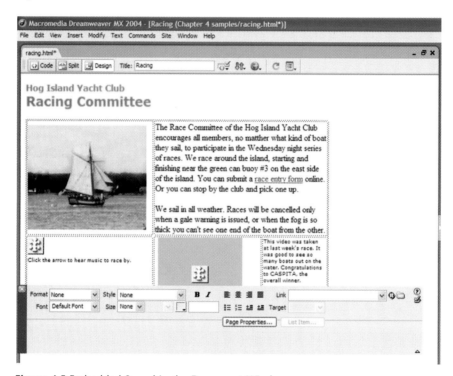

Figure 4.5 Embedded Sound in the Document Window

This gray square will not show in the user's browser. It is simply a placeholder for the embedded sound. If you do nothing else, the sound will begin to download as soon as the page opens, and will begin to play as soon as it has arrived. You'll learn in the next section how to change the way the sound appears, and how to let the user control its playing.

You can embed as many sounds as you like on a Web page, but be careful—when they all begin to play at once, the cacophony can be unbearable. It is wise to give the user some measure of control over the playing of the sound.

The best way to see how this works is to insert a sound, and then preview the page in your browser.

Linked Sound

Making a link to a sound is like any other kind of link in Dreamweaver: Select an object to link from, such as a word in the text, or an image, and then choose Modify→Make link from the menubar. Then use the dialog box to link to the sound file you need. To test the link, preview the page in your browser. Notice how the browser opens a new window to play the sound.

The opening of this new window takes the user's attention from your Web page, and can introduce unwanted graphic and design effects, as well as (for some players) unwanted advertising and promotion. Think twice before using linked sound in your site.

Play Sound Behavior

Dreamweaver offers an additional method for using sound on your Web page, through a Javascript behavior. This allows you to set a picture or a button so that it plays a sound when clicked. The sound will play in a new window, as with a linked sound. Here's how to do it:

1. Select an image or button on your Web page. (To insert a button, choose Insert→Form Objects→Button from the menubar, and set its action to *None* in the Properties Window.)

2. Choose Window→Behaviors from the menubar.

3. Click the behaviors tab.

4. Click the + in the Behaviors window to get a list of possible behaviors.

5. From this list, choose Play Sound.

6. Use the dialog box to navigate to the sound you need.

The Behaviors window will show that an onClick behavior has been attached to the selected object, as shown in Figure 4.6. Preview this page in the browser, and you will see (and hear) how the sound works.

Figure 4.6 Play Sound Behavior

Controlling Sound

Dreamweaver can help you to modify the way that the sound appears on the page, and to let the user control it. In most cases, it's a good idea to let your audience decide whether or not to hear the sounds on your page; rarely should you force them to listen to your music or your message without some way to shut it off or turn it down.

When you use linked sound, this control is built in; the user can simply close the new window that opens with the link. But for embedded sound, there's no control for the user unless you build it in.

The nature of the controls available to you (and your audience) depends on the format of the sound that is used. We cannot cover all of the possible controls of all of the different formats and players. But since the method of working with them in Dreamweaver is the same for all, we will use the QuickTime format in the examples. The control parameters for the other formats can be found on their sponsor's Web sites, which are listed at the end of this chapter. You can control whether the sound plays automatically or waits for the user's click; whether or not the sound displays a controller on the page; how big the controller appears; and other parameters. Table 4.5 lists some common parameters for sounds.

Table 4.5 Common User Control Parameters for Sounds

Parameter	Values	Result
Autoplay	True or false	Makes the sound begin playing as soon as the page is viewed.
Controller	True or false	Shows a slider that lets the user stop, start, advance, or rewind the sound.
Height	Measurement in pixels	Sets the height of the controller.
Hidden	True or false	Hides the file so it does not display.
Loop	True or false	Plays the sound over and over again.
Width	Measurement in pixels	Sets the width of the controller.

Set these parameters as follows:

1. Select the gray square that represents the sound on the Dreamweaver page.
2. Click the Parameters button in the Properties window.
3. Click the + button in the Parameters window to open a new field.
4. Type the name of a parameter into the field, such as *Autoplay*, or *Controller*.
5. Press Tab on the keyboard to open a field to enter the value for this parameter.
6. Enter a value into this field, such as *False* or *True*. (The actions so far would set the sound so it did not play until the user clicked the controller.)
7. Click OK to close the Parameters window.

A typical Parameters window for a sound might look like Figure 4.7.

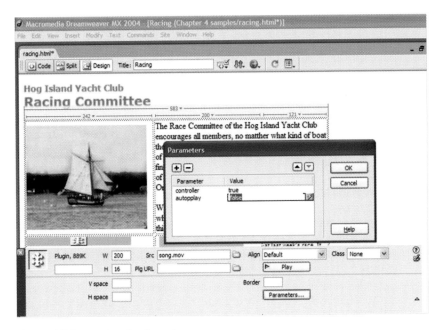

Figure 4.7 Parameters for Sound

The height and width of the controller can be set in the Properties window, as shown in Figure 4.7. The controller allows the user to stop, start, rewind, fast forward, and set the volume of the sound. You can insert several sounds on a Web page, each with its own controller. It's a good idea to indicate the nature of the sound in text next to the controller.

☆WARNING **Some Parameters Don't Apply**

Not all of the parameters mentioned here will work with all of the different file formats. And some formats may include parameters not listed here. Check the sites of the format owners, listed at the end of this chapter, to learn more about the possible parameters for each one.

Once you have set the parameters, you should preview the page in the browser to see and hear how it works.

☆WARNING **Sound on a Menu Page**

If you put a sound on a home page or a menu page—a page that you expect your users to return to again and again during their visit to your site—and set it to play automatically every time the page is viewed, you will end up with unhappy users. They will be forced to listen to that same sound play over and over every time they go back to the page. Save your sounds for situations where they truly help your purposes, and keep them off menu pages.

Working with Sound

◎◎ Working with Animation

As sound provokes the ear, animation captures the eye. People pay attention to motion on a Web page. Moving objects can help tell a story or explain a process. An animated diagram may explain a series of events better than any other media. Dreamweaver makes it easy to use animation—especially Fireworks and Flash animation—on a Web page. But, like sound, you must first prepare the animation outside of Dreamweaver, save it, and later insert the animation into a Dreamweaver document.

Preparing Animation

The two most common forms of animation found on the Web are animated GIF or PNG images and Flash movies. Animated GIFs can be created with Photoshop or with programs such as GIFBuilder and GIF Animator. Flash animations are created with Macromedia Flash. Macromedia Fireworks can prepare PNG animations that are very similar to GIF. You will find links to more information about these programs at the end of this chapter.

It's beyond the scope of this book to explain how to use these programs to create an animation. For an introduction to preparing animations in general, look at *The Web Wizard's Guide to Multimedia*. To get started with Flash, try *The Web Wizard's Guide to Flash*. The process of making an animation depends on which form you are using.

Making a GIF Animation

To build a GIF animation you first prepare a series of still images of the same size, one slightly different from the next, so that when they are displayed one after the other in rapid succession, they create the perception of movement. The images are most often prepared in an image-editing program such as Photoshop. Then you import these images into the GIF animating program; set the timing, transparence, looping, and other parameters; and save them in the animated GIF format. GIF animations are good for small moving logos and simple banner ads. All of the browsers can display animated GIFs without a plug-in. The animation is saved into the appropriate Web site folder with a .gif filename extension.

Fireworks Animation

Fireworks is best for small vector graphic animations of shapes. You draw the shapes directly in Fireworks, and then use Fireworks' tools to stretch, shrink, move, or rotate the shapes over time. Flash animations are saved in the Portable Network Graphics formation with the .png filename extension and are read by all the latest browsers without a plug-in.

Flash Animation

Flash is the most complete and most complex of the animation programs described here. It can help you create vector graphic animations that travel quickly over the Web and look good on the screen. *The Web Wizard's Guide to Flash* provides detailed information on creating Flash animations, much more than we can provide in this book. The process of creating animation with Flash works like this:

1. Create or import the graphic elements. Flash provides tools to draw shapes and text, and to set their colors. You can also import images from other sources. These graphic elements will appear on the *stage*, and also show in the *timeline*. For best results, put each item into its own *layer*.

2. Create *keyframes*. In the timeline, you set up the beginning and ending frames (called keyframes) of the animation of each element. The keyframes in Figure 4.8 are indicated with a black dot. The number of frames between the keyframes determines the length (in time) of the animation.

3. Modify the graphic elements in the keyframes. Animation involves some kind of movement or change over time. You can animate the object's location, rotation, transparency, or shape. This is done by setting these attributes in the two keyframes, one at the beginning of the sequence, and one at the end.

4. Insert a *motion tween*. This creates the intervening frames between the beginning and ending keyframes. In the timeline in Figure 4.8 you can see the motion tween indicated as an arrow that stretches between the keyframes.

5. Try the animation. By playing the frames in sequence, you can see how the animation works. You can also test the animation in the Flash Player at this time.

6. Modify the animation.

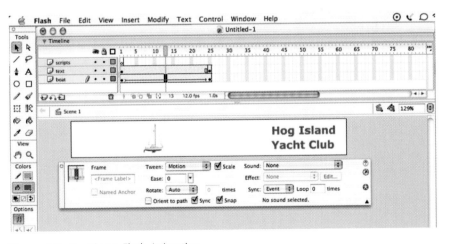

Figure 4.8 Creating a Flash Animation

No matter what your source of animation, make sure it is saved in your Web site folder, with a proper filename and extension.

Inserting Animation

All animations are added to the Dreamweaver document with the Insert menu item. If you are inserting a GIF or Fireworks (PNG) animation, use Insert→Image. For a Flash animation, use Insert→Media→Flash. The GIF and PNG animations will display their first frames in the Dreamweaver document window, while the Flash animation will appear as a gray rectangle.

To view the animation, use File→Preview in Browser.

Avoid changing the size of an animation by stretching or shrinking it in Dreamweaver. The results may not be as smooth or viewable as in their original size.

Controlling Animation

Dreamweaver provides no control over GIF or PNG animations; these will simply play in the browser in the manner in which they were created. If you want these types of animations to loop, this parameter must be set in the software you used to create the animation. For Flash animations, you can use Dreamweaver's Properties window to control the looping of the animation and determine whether it plays automatically or waits for the user to click on it.

Figure 4.9 Properties Window for Flash Animation

Combining Animation with Sound

An interesting effect can be achieved by combining a simple animation with a voice or music file on the same page. An example of this can be seen at `http://www.bu.edu/com/mcapr/ad/code/parenio.html`, which combines a GIF animation of photographs of a teacher, combined with her voice. This is accomplished by inserting both the sound and the animation as described above, and setting them both to play automatically as the page loads.

◎◎ Working with Video

Of all the multimedia types, video takes the most work to prepare and offers the largest number of choices for serving it from your site. Video files are gigantic, and require considerable crafty compression in order to be viewable on the Web. They sometimes require a particular type of server and special treatment if they are to be streamed in real time. All video requires a plug-in for the user's browser, as well as a good deal of bandwidth on the user's connection; acceptable video on a Web page calls for at least a DSL or cable modem connection.

Once it has been prepared, video can allow a Web site to do more for the viewer. Dreamweaver makes it easy to embed and control video on your Web pages.

Four different systems currently compete to provide the technologies for using video on the Web: RealPlayer, QuickTime, Windows Media Player, and Flash. All four work with both Macintosh and Windows operating systems, provide streaming as well as downloadable video, and offer good quality compression and performance. Up-to-date examples and specs on each system can be found in the online references listed at the end of this chapter.

In most cases, the video system you choose will depend on the server that you have available, the software at your disposal, and the competence of your webmaster. If your organization has licensed the RealPlayer server and uses the RealProducer software, then this might be your best choice. The same is true for the Windows Media Player. If you are working without a dedicated video server, then either Flash or QuickTime will be easier for you to use. And if you own a Macintosh with iMovie, then QuickTime is your best choice.

No matter which system you use, the process is the same:

1. Prepare the video with the software tools provided for the system you have chosen.

2. Save the video file either to the video server or to Web server.

3. Insert the video into a Dreamweaver document.

4. View the page containing the video within the browser to confirm its operation.

To make the best use of this section of the chapter, obtain a short video file in one of the formats described above. The Web Wizard Web site contains some sample video files for this purpose, which you can download. The video files are in the QuickTime (.mov) format, which will be easiest to use for now.

Preparing Video

Most Web developers use a video-editing program such as Adobe Premiere, iMovie, or Final Cut to capture video from its source; edit it, add titles, transitions, and narration as necessary; and save it in the format suitable for their audience. Many developers also use a compression program such as Discreet Cleaner or QuickTime Player Pro to further treat the video for optimal performance on the Web. The selection and use of video editing programs is beyond the scope of this book, but in most cases the program you choose depends on the video system you plan to use. The online references at the end of this chapter refer you to the sources of detailed information on each of the products currently available. Table 4.6 shows typical editors and compressors for various video platform choices.

Table 4.6 Video Editing and Compression Tools

Video System	Editor	Compressor	File Format	Method
RealVideo	Adobe Premiere, Pinnacle Studio 8	Real Producer, Discreet Cleaner	.rm or .ra	Linked only
QuickTime	iMovie, Final Cut, Premiere	QuickTime Player Pro, Discreet Cleaner	.mov	Embedded or Linked
Windows Media	Windows Movie Maker, Pinnacle Studio 8	Windows Media Encoder	.asf	Linked only
Flash	Premiere, iMovie, Final Cut	Flash, Sorenson Spark	.swf	Embedded or Linked

☆ **TIP**   Linked or Embedded?

Video can appear within the context of a Web page, right next to the text and images; this is called *embedded* video. The video can also be *linked* to the page, so that when the link is clicked, the video opens in its own player window, outside of the Web page. Dreamweaver lets you set up either method.

As you save your video from the editor or compressor, you will choose the type and amount of compression to apply. The more you compress the data, the faster it will arrive at your user's browser, but the lower its quality will be. You should do some trial-and-error testing to find the best compression for your needs. *The Web Wizard's Guide to Multimedia* can provide more help on editing and compressing video files.

Although other video formats such as AVI can be used on the Web and with Dreamweaver, this uncompressed format has been superseded by the newer and more efficient formats that are listed in Table 4.6.

Pixel Size

The number of pixels in the video image determines in large measure the size and data rate of the file. A video of 320 × 240 pixels is about the largest that can be received comfortably by most users. To conserve data rate and file size, consider reducing the size of the video to 240 × 180 pixels, or even 160 × 120 pixels for modem users. Once you have made a choice, do not stretch or shrink the pixel size. Keep it at the original dimensions. Make a note of the dimensions of your video image; you'll need them when it is time to insert the video into Dreamweaver.

Frame Rate

The frame rate also has a large effect on file size and data rate. For most Web video, 12 frames per second (fps) is acceptable. You might use 15 fps for video with more motion, and 10 fps for talking heads. Contrary to what you might think, a faster frame rate will under most circumstances cause a decrease in performance, as the increased data rate gums up the works and sends viewers more information than they can receive.

Data Rate

After you have prepared your video files, check their *data rate* against the capabilities of your audience. Don't use large, high-bandwidth videos with an audience connecting mostly through modems. A DSL subscriber with a bandwidth of 300 kilobits per second will not be able to receive a streamed video file with a data rate of more than 300 kbps. In fact, the data rate of your video should be kept well under the nominal bandwidth of your users. Experience has taught us that a bandwidth of under 200 kbps works best with DSL and cable connections.

You can check your data rate by dividing the file size of the video by its length. A 1.3 megabyte file 30 seconds long has an average data rate of about 350 kbps (1.3 megabytes/30 seconds = 43 Kilobytes per second = 350 kilobits per second). You may also examine the data rate with the software used for compression, under Movie Statistics or Movie Properties.

Download or Stream?

Video can be received by the audience in three ways:

☆ *Complete file download.* Here the video file is transferred from the Web server to the viewer's hard disk, in the same way as an image or text file. When the entire file has been received, the video begins to play. This method is best for small, short videos less than one megabyte in size and is used only with certain QuickTime and RealPlayer .rm files. For this method, the data rate is irrelevant; it's the size of the file that matters.

☆ *Progressive download.* In this method the video file downloads to the user's hard disk, but begins playing as soon as enough video has arrived. It's used with QuickTime video (where it is called Fast Start Streaming), Flash video .swf files, and RealPlayer .rm files. Here the data rate is significant, and should be less than the viewer's bandwidth. Progressive download does not require a special video streaming server—the files can be served from a standard Web server.

☆ *Real-time streaming.* In this method the video information never reaches the viewer's hard drive; instead it is played in real time, frame by frame, as soon as it arrives, and then disappears. This method is used in RealPlayer .ra files, and with QuickTime Streaming video, the Flash Communication Server, and Windows Media Player. Data rate is critical to good performance, and a special video streaming server is required.

More information on each of these methods and technologies can be found in the online references at the end of this chapter.

For most beginning Web developers, QuickTime or Flash video, in the progressive download method, are easiest to work with because they are identical across platforms and require no special streaming server. We will use these two methods in our examples.

☆ *QuickTime.* To prepare a QuickTime video, use QuickTime Player Pro, Discreet Cleaner, iMovie, or Final Cut software to export the file in the QuickTime Fast Start streaming format, with the .mov filename extension.

☆ *Flash.* To prepare a Flash video, import the video into a Flash document, and then export the file as a Flash movie with the .swf filename extension.

No matter which method you use, make sure the video is saved in your Web site folder with a Web-legal filename and the proper filename extension.

Inserting Video

Dreamweaver makes it easy to embed a video into a Web page. For QuickTime video, follow these steps:

1. Place the cursor at the spot on the page where you want the video to appear. This can be either on a new line of text or inside a cell of a table.

2. Choose Insert→Media→Plug-in from the menubar. There is no listing in the menu for video per se; video is considered by Dreamweaver to be a medium that requires a plug-in.

3. Watch the video appear on the page as a small gray square with a plug-in icon, as shown in Figure 4.10.

4. Expand the icon to match the pixel size of your video image. If you plan to include a controller, add 16 pixels to the vertical dimension.

5. Test the video by previewing the page in the browser.

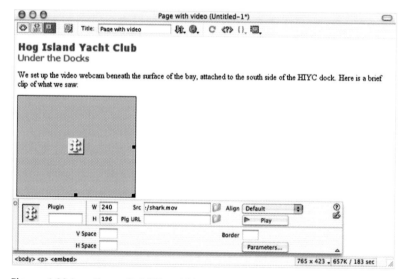

Figure 4.10 Inserting a QuickTime Video

For Flash video, follow these steps:

1. Place the cursor at the spot on the page where you want the video to appear. This can be either on a new line of text or inside a cell of a table.

2. Choose Insert→Media→Flash from the menubar.

3. Watch the flash video appear on the page as a gray rectangle with a Flash icon.

4. Test the video by previewing the page in the browser.

Linking to a Video

You can also link a video to a Web page, so that it opens in its own separate video player window. Follow these steps:

1. Create something to link from on the Web page. This may be a word or phrase in the text, or an image.

2. Select the item you want to link from.

3. Choose Modify→Make Link from the menubar.

4. Browse to the video file (if it's in your Web folder), or enter the URL of the video (if it's on a RealPlayer server).

5. Click OK.

6. Check the link by previewing the Web page in the browser.

☆**WARNING** Plug-in

If your browser does not have the right plug-in or player, you won't see the video. Each system of video requires its own plug-in. You can download these players from the URLs listed at the end of this chapter.

Controlling Video

Dreamweaver lets you exert a measure of control over how the embedded video appears, and what the user can do with it. Use the Properties window to set the parameters for the video. If you follow the directions above, the video will appear on the page and begin playing automatically without user intervention. And if it's a Flash video, it will also play over and over in a loop because that is the default setting.

To change the playback parameters for a QuickTime video, select the video rectangle on the Web page, then click the Parameters button in the Properties window. In the dialog box that appears, enter the name of the parameter in the left column, and its desired value in the right. Some of the parameters that can be set are shown in Table 4.7.

To change the parameters for a Flash video, select the Flash rectangle in the Web page, then use the Properties window to check or uncheck the Autoplay and Loop parameters.

Test the results of your parameter setting by previewing the page in the browser.

Table 4.7 Some QuickTime Video Parameters

Parameter	Values	Result
Autoplay	True or false	Makes the video begin playing as soon as the page is viewed.
Controller	True or false	Shows a slider that lets the user stop, start, advance, or rewind the video.
Height	Measurement in pixels	Sets the height of the video including its controller.
Loop	True or false	Plays the video over and over again.
Width	Measurement in pixels	Sets the width of the video.

◎◎ Multimedia in Dreamweaver

Animation, sound, and video take some work to produce, but they can add extra power to a Web site. Like the spinnaker on a sailboat, multimedia can take your users along the desired course faster and with more excitement. Dreamweaver provides tools that make it easy to include the multimedia items in your site.

☆ Summary

▷ Dreamweaver can recognize and provide all the necessary code to include a wide range of multimedia file types in your Web pages.

▷ The bandwidth and plug-ins used by your audience will determine the nature and extent of the multimedia that you include in your Web site.

▷ Dreamweaver can embed sound in a Web page, but the sound file must first be carefully compressed and saved in a proper format for reception by the audience.

▷ GIF or Flash animations, prepared outside of Dreamweaver, may be inserted onto a Web page using functions provided with Dreamweaver.

▷ Video files must be carefully prepared and compressed with QuickTime, Flash, RealPlayer, or Windows Media tools. Then they can be embedded in or linked to Web pages using Dreamweaver.

☆ Online References

Information on compressing media files with Discreet Cleaner
http://www.discreet.com/products/cleaner/

Reviews on video editing software
http://www.techtv.com/callforhelp/products/story/
0,24330,3329928,00.html

Video editing with Pinnacle Video Studio 8
http://www.pinnaclesys.com/

Video specifications and software tools in Apple's QuickTime
http://www.apple.com/quicktime

Video information and software tools in RealPlayer
http://www.realnetworks.com

Information and software tools in Flash and Fireworks
http://www.macromedia.com

Video information and software tools in Windows Media
http://www.microsoft.com

☆ Review Questions

1. List at least five media types that Dreamweaver can import, and explain the software tools used to produce each type.

2. Explain the role of bandwidth, and of plug-ins, in the reception of multimedia material on a Web page.

3. Trace the steps in preparing an animation, and in inserting the animation into a Dreamweaver document.

4. List the factors you must consider as you prepare sound files for use with Dreamweaver.

5. Explain the difference between embedded and linked media in a Dreamweaver Web page.

6. Trace the process of preparing a video file for use in Dreamweaver, and of embedding the file in a Web page.

7. Explain how the appearance and user control of sound and video files can be accomplished with Dreamweaver.

☆ Hands-On Exercises

1. Examine a Web site that contains lots of multimedia. List the animations, sounds, and videos, and describe the nature and purpose of each one.

2. Go to the Web sites of Macromedia, RealNetworks, Apple Computer, and Microsoft, and check to see if you have the latest plug-ins and players for Flash, RealPlayer, QuickTime, and Windows Media. Download the latest players as necessary.

3. Prepare a simple animation with either Flash or a GIF animation program. Insert the animation onto a Web page with Dreamweaver, and test its operation with a browser.

4. Prepare or obtain a sound file suitable for delivery over the Web. Embed this sound into a Dreamweaver document, and provide a controller for the user. Test the document with a Web browser.

5. Prepare or obtain a short video file in one of the formats described in this chapter. Embed the video in a Web page with Dreamweaver, provide a controller, and test the page in a Web browser.

6. Assemble a simple Web site that contains text, images, animation, sound, and video.

WORKING WITH FORMS

Get Data from the Instruments

The Web site that we have built so far, with text, images, and multimedia, may do a good job getting information to the audience. But what if you want information back *from* them? After all, the Web is a two-way street—your viewers can send data to you as well as receive it from you. This chapter shows you how to create a *form* in which your audience can enter information, make choices and selections, and then submit this data to you. You have seen and used forms on the Web if you have ever signed up for a service or purchased a product. Dreamweaver makes this easy to do. It's like getting feedback from your instruments in a sailboat: How deep is the water? How fast is the wind? How fast is the boat? Forms can put you in closer touch with what your audience is thinking, and allow them to tell you what they need.

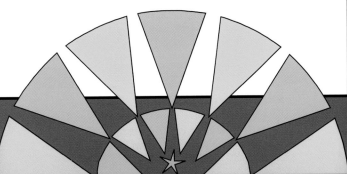

◎◎ Chapter Objectives

☆ To understand how forms work on the Web and in Dreamweaver

☆ To learn how to design a form that will get you the information you need

☆ To find out how to set up a form on a Web page, and to define the form action

☆ To be able to insert various form elements, such as text fields, buttons, check boxes, and menus

☆ To learn how to test the operation of the form in a browser, and to receive the results

◎◎ How Forms Work in Dreamweaver

The Purpose of a Form

Forms on Web pages can serve many different functions. A form can let someone sign up for an event, such as the registration form for the Summer Music Institute shown in Figure 5.1.

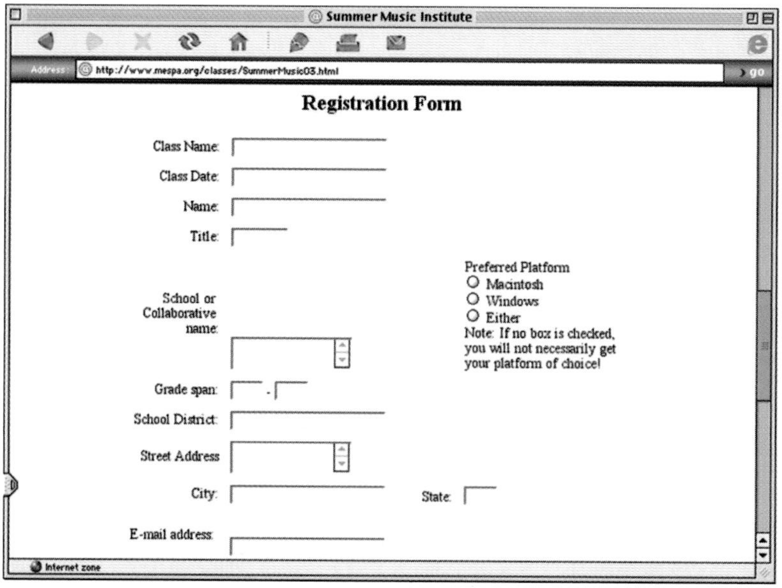

Figure 5.1 Registration Form

Forms can collect comments or feedback from the audience, as shown in the technical support feedback form shown in Figure 5.2.

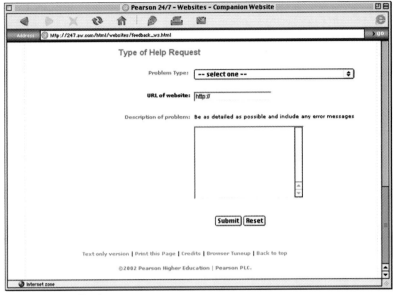

Figure 5.2 Feedback Form

Forms can gather information from the audience to create a database, as shown in Figure 5.3.

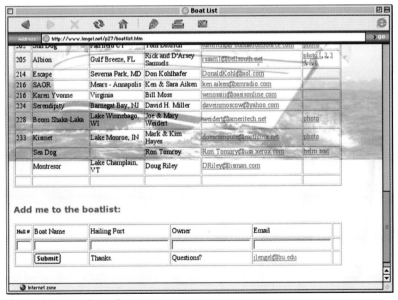

Figure 5.3 Data Entry Form

Forms can collect the information necessary to enable a customer to order and purchase a product, as illustrated in Figure 5.4.

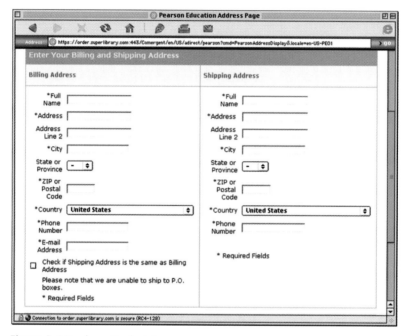

Figure 5.4 Purchase Product Form

Forms can collect data from respondents to a survey or poll, as shown in Figure 5.5.

And everyone is familiar with forms that allow you to submit keywords to a search engine or database, as shown in Figure 5.6.

The purpose of all of these forms is twofold:

☆ To collect information from the audience: words typed in, boxes checked, or selections made from a list.

☆ To send this information over the Web to a recipient. The recipient might be a person who gets the information as an email, or it might be a database, which adds the information as a new record.

If you are building your own sample Web site as you work through this book, think of an opportunity to collect some information from your audience. As you advance along the steps of building a form, create a simple form for your Web site that collects this information. Since the building of a database is beyond the scope of this book, you'll create a form that sends the data back to you as an email. For your first attempt, consider a simple form that collects four or five pieces of information.

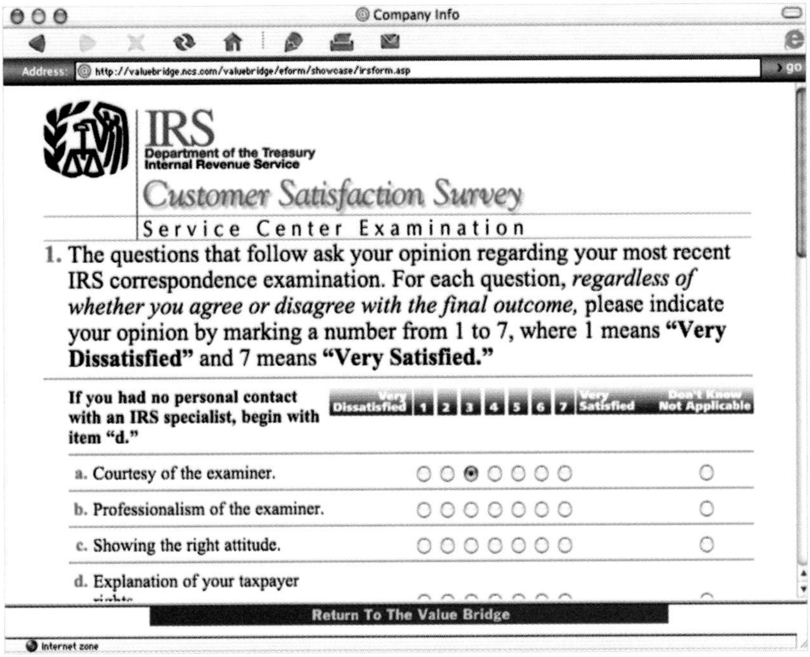

Figure 5.5 Online Survey Form

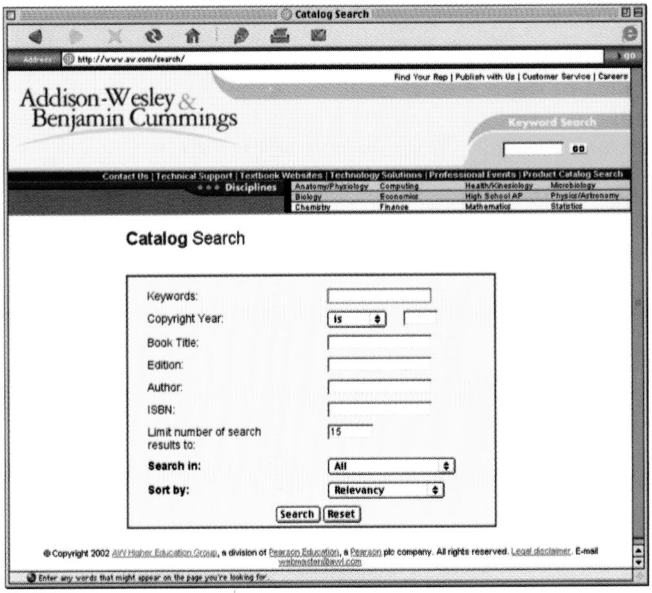

Figure 5.6 Search Terms Entry Form

Designing a Form

☆**WARNING Not e-Commerce**

The form you build as you work through this chapter is less complex than the forms used by commercial Web sites for the selection and purchase of products. Those forms communicate with a set of databases on the company's Web server—they send data to a program on the server that knows exactly where to put the data that the user submits. Your form will be simpler in design and functionality, sending its data to your email account.

The Steps in Building a Form

Dreamweaver's tools make it easy to create a form, but a little advance planning is required before you sit down and start inserting fields and buttons. The rest of this chapter takes you through each of these six steps in detail:

1. Design the form. Determine the information you need to collect, how you'll label it and lay it out on the page, and how the data will be handled when it is submitted.

2. Insert the form onto a Web page. Use Dreamweaver's tools to create a form area and define the form action.

3. Insert form elements. Insert the text fields, radio buttons, check boxes, and popup menus you need to collect the information.

4. Insert a Submit button.

5. Optional: Construct a script to allow the processing of the information.

6. Test the form in a browser, and make sure the information is received.

The first step takes the longest. It deserves most of your attention, and will determine the success of your form. The next three steps involve lots of technical details, and must be performed carefully. And the last step is where you find out if the form works. In many cases, you will find yourself working back and forth between steps three and five as you perfect your form.

☆**WARNING Browser Email Preferences**

When you test your form in the browser, it will not send data unless its email preferences are set properly. To set them, go to the Preferences panel of your browser, and enter your email address and the URL of your email sending server.

◎◎ Designing a Form

You don't need Dreamweaver to design your form. It's better to use pencil and paper, a word-processor, or a spreadsheet. At this point you define the purpose of your form, describe each piece of data, decide where to send the results, and determine how the various elements will appear on the page.

Define the Purpose

As you saw in the examples at the beginning of this chapter, a form can have a variety of purposes. What will be the purpose of your form? What exactly are you trying to accomplish? What information do you need to gather? To help you determine the purpose of your form, answer these questions:

☆ Why are you collecting these data?

☆ Exactly what information do you need to collect?

☆ How will you use the information you collect?

☆ **WARNING** **Data Privacy**

Many people are concerned about the amount of data that is collected from them on the Web, and the ways it is used. So be careful. Collect only the data you need from your viewers; tell them why you're collecting it and exactly how you will use it. Europeans seem to be even more wary than Americans, and have passed laws that regulate how and why you can collect data on your Web site. If your site's audience includes members of the European Community, you should take a look at the article listed in the online references at the end of this chapter.

Describe the Fields

We'll call each piece of information that you plan to collect a *field*. This word comes from the world of databases, where each item in a *record* is called a *field*. For instance, if I sign up online for a sailboat race, I create a new record for my entry; its fields include my first name, my last name, the name of my boat, the length of my boat, and its handicap rating. This record contains five fields.

Make a list of each of the pieces of information you plan to collect with your form. For each field, assign a label, a field name, the possible choices, and a reason for collecting it, as shown in Table 5.1.

Table 5.1 Defining the Fields

Label	Field Name	Choices	Input Type	Reason
First Name	firstname	Text, no limit	Text field	Identification of skipper
Last Name	lastname	Text, no limit	Text field	Identification of skipper
Club Member	membership	Yes, No	Radio Buttons (member)	Determine entry fee
Name of Boat	boatname	Text, no limit	Text field	Identification of boat
Type of Boat	boattype	Sloop, Ketch, Yawl, Schooner, Other	Popup list	Classification of entry
Length of Boat	boatlength	Number, 2 digits	Text field	Classification of entry
PHRF Rating	phrf	Number, 3 digits	Text field	Classification of entry
Social Events	social	Lunch, Reception, Supper	Check boxes (social)	Planning for food service

Even though you may not be setting up a database for this project, it's good practice to spell out the items in your form in this way. You'll need the information from this table when you set up your form in Dreamweaver.

In Table 5.1, the *Label* of the item is what the user will see on the page. The *Field Name* is what will be sent back to you with the data; the user will not see this word. The *Choices* list the possible entries for this field. The *Input Type* determines the type of HTML form object that you will use for this item. And the rightmost column is where you make note of the *Reason* for collecting this item.

Collect exactly the items you need, no more, and no less. Make sure that the labels you choose will be understandable by the audience, so that there will be no question about what the user is supposed to enter. Keep your field names simple, using single words without spaces or punctuation, as shown in Table 5.1. These kinds of field names will travel well over the Web. If you were building a database to collect this information, these field names would match exactly the names of the fields in the database.

☆**WARNING Too Much Data!**

It's so easy to add another field to a form that we often make the mistake of collecting information we don't need. Your audience will appreciate your limiting your form to only essential items, making it easy to complete.

Guide to Types of Input

Notice that some of the information in this form is collected in a text field, some with round radio buttons, some with square check boxes, and some with a popup menu. These are all different *form objects* that can be used to collect data. Other form objects in Dreamweaver include text area, button, file field, image field, and hidden field. It's very important to choose the right type of form object to match the kind of input you want from the viewer.

For names, addresses, zip codes, and other text or numerical information that the user will enter from the keyboard free-form—where they can type in any letters or numbers they want—it's proper to use a *text field* (if it's a word or two) or a *text area* (if it's more than a sentence).

When you want to force your users to make a choice between a few mutually exclusive options, such as gender (male or female) or type of boat (sloop or yawl or ketch), then it's proper to use a *radio button*. When you click one of the radio buttons in a series, the others go off, just as when you select stations on a car radio. Users can see all of the possible choices on the screen without clicking, but must select only one.

If you want to provide a list of choices and let the user select more than one of them, then use *check boxes*. In the example above, the entrants in the sailboat race can order lunch, a reception, supper, some meals, or nothing at all.

If you want to provide a longer list of items for the user to choose one from, such as credit card type (Visa, MasterCard, American Express, or Discover) or state of residence (list of 50 states), then you'd insert a *List/Menu* type of input in the form. This is called a popup list in the example above. The user cannot see all of the choices in a List/menu until she clicks the menu.

The other types of form objects are seldom used in simple Web sites, but you can learn more about them by connecting to the online references listed at the end of this chapter.

For each piece of information you want to collect, you should determine which type of form object to use. Sometimes the choice is clear, as with name or gender. But for other data in your list, you could just as well use a series of radio buttons as a popup menu. Your decision will depend on the number of choices you want to show and the size and layout of the form.

Determine the Recipient

Where will the data be sent when the user clicks the *Submit* or *Send* button that you will put at the bottom of your form? Will it be added to a database on a database server somewhere? Or will it be sent to you as an email?

If you want the data to go into a database, then you need to set up the database on a Web server. Web database design is beyond the scope of this book, but Macromedia's ColdFusion software can work with Dreamweaver and a standard database server so that you can build forms that send their data to a database. The steps in this process include:

1. Design the database. Determine the records and fields, and the data types for each field. Create the database, using software such as FileMaker, MySQL, Access, or 4D.

2. Run the database on a Web server. Make a note of the URL of the database.

3. Use ColdFusion and Dreamweaver together to link the form elements on the Web page to the fields of the database.

4. Test the form in a browser.

See the online references at the end of this chapter for more information on this topic.

For your first form, it's easier to send the information from the Web page to your own email account. This is very easy to set up and to test. You need to know your email address, and you need to make sure that your Web browser preferences are set up to send email.

Design the Layout

A form that's well laid out will be easier for your viewers to understand and use. Look at the two forms illustrated in Figure 5.7. Which will be easier to use?

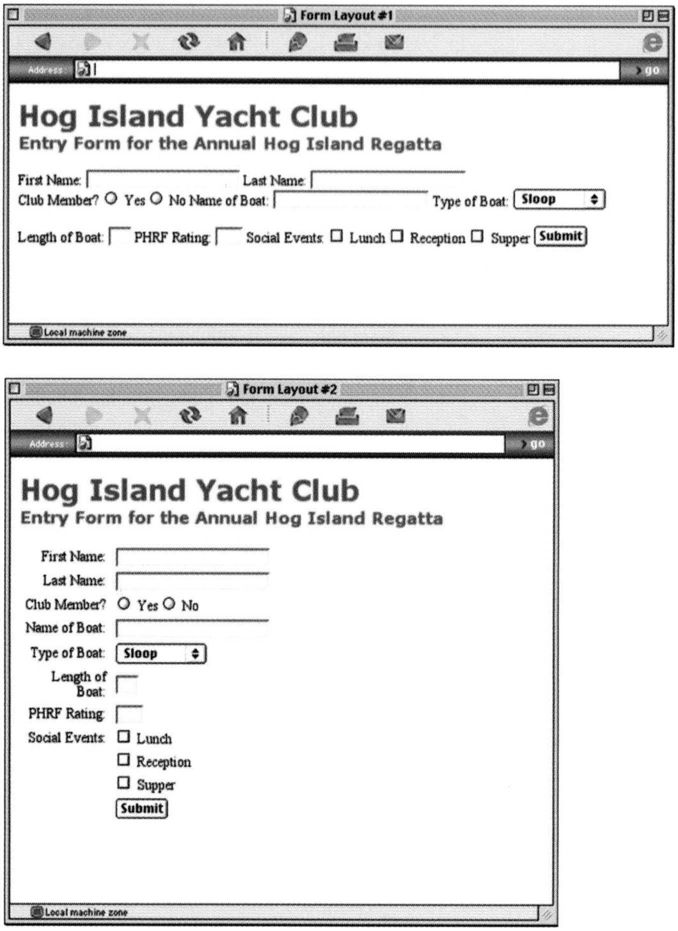

(a)

(b)

Figure 5.7 Sample Form Layouts

Figure 5.7(a) seems scattered around the screen, and it's difficult to tell which label goes with which item. It's also hard to be sure you've filled out all of the information. Figure 5.7(b) lines up the labels and the items in a consistent manner that helps the user keep track of the information requested. Sketch the layout of your form with pencil and paper, in a way that makes it easy for your audience to use. Pay careful attention to the alignment of the items, and the positions of the labels and the input objects. If all of the input fields and buttons are in a single line, it is easier to move from one to the next, and to make sure they are all filled in. If each label is placed next to only one input item, there'll be no confusion as to which label goes with which input item.

Avoid adding unnecessary design or layout elements in the form, such as decorative images, boxes, lines, and flourishes. These distract the user from the function of filling out the form. But remember that images may be useful as part of a form, such as small drawings of the various types of boats in the example shown above. These kinds of functional images may help the novice user to more easily complete the form.

Write the Instructions

Some forms are self-explanatory, and need little by way of instructions or introduction. The entry form shown in Figure 5.7(b) needs only a title for the user to understand the purpose of the form and to know what to fill in. But many forms will need a bit more explanation. Each form on a Web site should make clear to the user:

☆ What is the purpose of the form?

☆ What information needs to go in each input item?

☆ Where will the information be sent when it is submitted?

☆ Where can I get further information on filling out the form?

This information can be incorporated into the title of the form, in an introductory paragraph, or in a footnote. As part of the planning process, you should compose the title, the instructions, and any necessary explanations, making them ready for pasting into the form in Dreamweaver.

◎◎ Setting Up the Form

Once the form is planned, you can open Dreamweaver and begin building it. First you'll set up the page that contains the form, then you'll insert the form, and finally you'll set its *action*. The form action is what happens to the data when the user submits the form.

Set Up the Page

Some forms are small enough to be incorporated into an existing Web page. The race entry form shown in Figure 5.7(b) might easily fit at the bottom of the page that announces the race. Longer forms should in most cases be placed on their own separate page.

☆ **TIP**   **Printing Forms**

Many Web users will print the form that you create. Even though they don't need to in most cases, some people like to review the form on paper, hand it on to an assistant for completion, or save a hard copy of their responses. And a few people whose browsers can't send email may find that the only way to submit the information is on paper. So set up your form for easy printing. Put it on a separate page. Avoid colored backgrounds or images—use plain black text on a white background.

Before you insert the form, set up the Web page by entering a heading, such as *July 4 Race Entry Form* or *Online Application Form* or *Product Order Form*. Make sure that the organization publishing the form is named somewhere on the page. Insert any introductory explanations or instructions, and enter these as text in Dreamweaver, as described in Chapter Two.

Insert the Form

On a new line just under the instructions, insert your form area by choosing Insert→Form from the menubar. At this point, your display will look something like Figure 5.8.

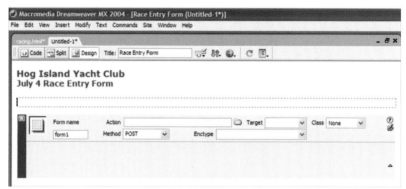

Figure 5.8 Inserting the Form Area

> ☆**WARNING**   **Invisibles**
>
> Can't see the red dotted outline of your form area? That's because it's invisible—your viewers won't be able to see it either. But you need to see it to create your form. Choose View→Visual Aids→Invisible Elements from the menubar, and you'll be able to see the red line that marks the edge of the form area.

Make sure your Properties window is open, as shown in Figure 5.8, and that the cursor is within the red form area. This red line sets the boundaries of the form. Any form objects placed within the form area will be sent along when the user clicks the Submit button.

Set the Form Action

In the form Properties window, enter a name for this form and an action. The action tells the browser where to send the information. Figure 5.9 shows two form actions, one that sends the information to the author as an email, and the other that sends it to a database.

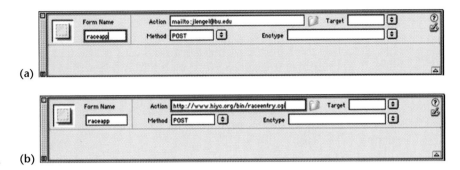

Figure 5.9 Setting the Form Action

The form action code for the emailed information is for example

```
mailto:jlengel@bu.edu
```

Notice that there are no spaces in the form action. The mailto: action is an HTML command that tells the browser to send the contents of the form by email to the address that follows. If you are building your own site, enter your own email address.

The form action to send to a database is for example

```
http://www.hiyc.org/bin/raceentry.cgi
```

This sends an HTTP (HyperText Transfer Protocol) command to the Hog Island Yacht Club Web server, which sends the information to a database. This is accomplished in this example through a CGI (Common Gateway Interface) script that instructs the server how to enter the contents of the form into the database. Since the example here is hypothetical, and the HIYC, its Web server, and its database do not exist, the code listed here will not work. So for your own project, it's best to use the email example shown above.

Every form needs a form action for it to work, and it's best to set it just after you insert the form area. You can go back and change the form action by clicking on the red line that defines the edge of the form and entering new text into the Action field in the Properties window.

⊚⊚ Inserting Form Elements

Now that your form is set up and its action established, you can enter its elements. For a simple form with no special layout needs, you can begin entering the labels and objects directly. For a more complex form, you'll want to set up a layout table.

Set Up a Layout Table

If your form is large enough to need formatting, it's best to set up the layout table first, and then insert the form objects into the cells of the table. For instance, to build the form shown in Figure 5.7(b), you'd start by inserting a table with 11 rows and two columns. Then you'd enter the labels into the left column, and the corresponding form objects into the right column, following the instructions below. When all are inserted, you'd align all the labels to the right to achieve the neat alignment shown in the illustration. Figure 5.10 shows the layout table for this example.

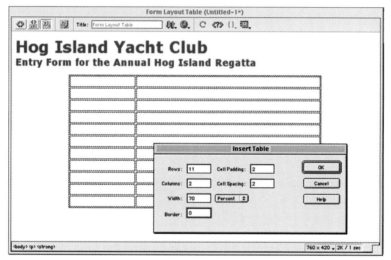

Figure 5.10 Setting Up a Layout Table

For a small and simple form, you may not need such a table—you can simply type the labels and insert the form objects directly into the page.

Insert a Text Field

For the entry of a name, a street, or other brief text information, use a *Text Field*. A text field is a form object that provides one line of information, as wide as you can fit on your page. To insert a text field:

1. Place the cursor where you want the field to appear.

2. Type the label for this field from the keyboard.

3. Insert the text field by choosing Insert→Form Objects→Text Field from the menubar.

4. See the text field appear in its default width of 24 characters.

5. In its Properties window, enter a name for this form object, as shown in Figure 5.11. (The name that you enter in the Properties window will not be seen by

the user, but will be submitted along with the data the user enters. This name may be, but need not be, the same as the label that the user sees. If you were feeding the data into a database, the name of the text field would match exactly one of the field names in the database.)

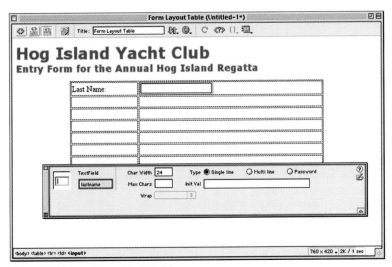

Figure 5.11 Inserting a Text Field

Insert a Text Area

If your users will be entering several sentences of text, then it's better to insert a *Text Area* that provides several lines for their comments. Choose Insert→Form Objects→Textarea from the menubar. In its Properties window, assign it a name, a width, and the number of lines to show. This creates a scrolling text field that will accommodate as much information as the user wants to enter.

Insert Radio Buttons

Radio buttons are used to select only one item from a list of choices. In most cases, you should place the radio button to the left of its label, as shown in Figure 5.7(b). Choose Insert→Form Object→Radio Button from the menubar. In its Properties window, you must enter a *name* and a *value* for each radio button.

☆ The *name* of a radio button indicates the category of data you are collecting. In the example shown in Figure 5.12, we are finding out whether the entrant is a member of the club, so we name this a *member* radio button.

☆ The *value* of a radio button indicates the choice the user has made. In this example, the value is set to yes. If the user chooses this button, the form will send the message "member = yes."

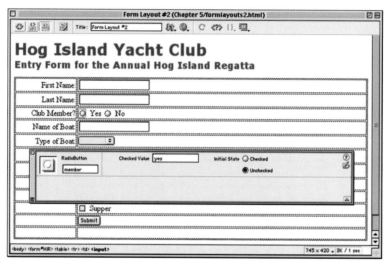

Figure 5.12 Inserting a Radio Button

The other radio buttons in this same category will be assigned the same name. For example, the *No* button shown in Figure 5.12 will be assigned the name *member* and the value *no*. This is shown in Figure 5.13.

Figure 5.13 Names and Values of Radio Buttons

The names of all of the radio buttons in a series must be exactly the same. It is through these names that the user's browser knows to make these forced-choice buttons that click off when another in the series is clicked on. The names are the same, but the values should be different. And of course, each series of radio buttons in a form needs to be assigned a different name.

The label for each radio button should be typed into the Dreamweaver document right after the button itself.

Insert Check Boxes

Check boxes look like radio buttons, except that they are square and they work differently. A user can select as many check boxes as she likes in the series, but with radio buttons only one choice is possible. Check boxes let the user choose none, one, some, or all of the items in the list. In the example shown in Figure 5.7(b), the user can sign up for lunch, the reception, or supper, or all three, or any two, or take no meals at all. As with radio buttons, the *names* of all the check boxes in a series are the same, but the *values* are different.

To insert a check box, choose Insert→Form Objects→Check Box from the menubar, and then complete the Properties window as shown in Figure 5.14.

Figure 5.14 Inserting a Check Box

As with radio buttons, the label for each box should be typed next to it.

Insert a Popup Menu

The popup menu shown in Figure 5.7(b) lets the user choose the type of boat from a menu of six choices. Its function is similar to that of a radio button in that only one choice can be made from the list, but the choices cannot be seen until the user clicks on the menu. This saves space on the page, but makes some information invisible to the user at the outset.

To create a popup menu, first type the label, and then choose Insert→Form Objects→List/Menu from the menubar. You will see a blank popup menu. In its Properties window, assign this menu a *name* and enter its *values*. In the example shown in Figure 5.15, the name of the menu is *boattype* and the possible values are *Sloop, Yawl, Ketch, Schooner, Catboat,* and *Cutter*.

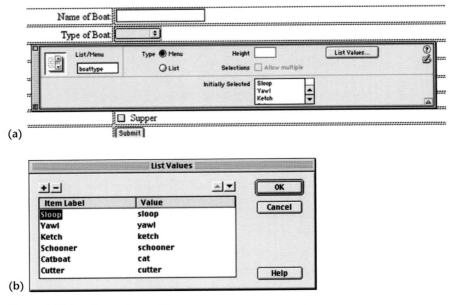

(a)

(b)

Figure 5.15 Inserting a Popup Menu

You can type the name of the menu directly into its Properties window. To enter the values, click the List Values... button in the upper right of the Properties window (Figure 5.15(a)) to open a window where you can enter the *Item Label* (what the viewer sees) and a *Value* (what gets sent upon submission) for each choice, as shown in Figure 5.15(b). Click the + button to add more labels.

☆**WARNING**   **Testing Form Objects in Dreamweaver**

Form objects do not work in the Dreamweaver environment in the same way that they do in the browser. The radio buttons don't select, and the popup menus don't pop. To see how the form object you just created will look and operate, you must preview the page in the browser by choosing File➔Preview in Browser from the menubar.

The List *Form Object*

Similar to a popup menu is a *list* form object. Use a list when you want the user to be able to choose more than one item from a scrolling list of choices. In the example shown here, we could have used a list to let the users choose which social events to attend. The functionality of a list is similar to that of a series of check boxes.

To make a list form object, follow the instructions for making a popup menu, but select the List button, and check off *Allow multiple* in the Selections box, as shown in Figure 5.16.

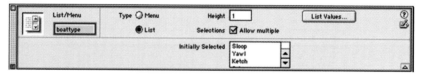

Figure 5.16 Inserting a List Form Object

Insert a Submit Button

Every form needs a Submit button. It need not say "submit"—any word can be used—but there must be a button that the user clicks to send the contents of the form to the recipient. In most cases, the Submit button is placed at the bottom of the form. Be careful to insert it inside the form area that's outlined in red.

To insert a Submit button, choose Insert➔Form Objects➔Button. You will see a Submit button appear. In its Properties window, you can change its label as necessary, perhaps to something more specific and less demeaning than *Submit*, such as *Send Form* or *Enter My Boat* or *Purchase Now*. Figure 5.17 shows this Properties window.

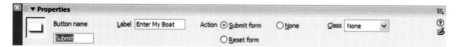

Figure 5.17 Insert Submit Button

By the same method, you can also create a second button that resets the form and clears out anything the user has entered. Follow the instructions for creating a Submit button, but in its Properties window click the *Reset* button.

Other Form Objects

In Dreamweaver's list of possible form objects, there are five additional possibilities that are seldom used by beginning Web developers. They are:

☆ *File field*—lets the user choose a file from his own computer that will be uploaded to the recipient of the form. This might be used to let the viewer send a picture of his boat to the race committee.

☆ *Image field*—creates a defined area for an image, most often drawn from a database, to be displayed on the Web page.

☆ *Hidden field*—creates a field on the page, not seen by the user, with a name and a value that's sent along to the recipient.

☆ *Radio Group*—makes it easier to set up a series of radio buttons for a single category in one step.

☆ *Jump menu*—creates a popup menu that links to another URL.

All of these can be inserted in similar fashion to the other types of form objects.

◎◎ Testing the Form

You cannot see what your form looks like or how it operates until you preview the page in a browser. Choose File➔Preview in Browser➔(name of browser), and watch your form appear. Test it as if you were a typical member of your site's audience. Check all the possibilities. Fill in the fields and select the buttons and boxes. Are all of the labels clear? Are items aligned for ease of use? Will the user know immediately which form object goes with which label? Is there enough room to type all the required information?

When the form is complete, click the Submit button. If you have set up your browser's email preferences as described earlier in this chapter, the data from the form should be sent in an email to the recipient you listed in the form action. If you are the recipient, wait a few minutes, and then check your email. You should see a new message in the In Box, containing the contents of the form. The message will look something like Figure 5.18.

Figure 5.18 Form Output Via Email

Revise the Form

Seldom does a Web form work perfectly on the first try. The alignment may need cleaning up. The labels may need to be rewritten to be clearer to the audience. The radio buttons may not function as desired. The Form Action may have been set incorrectly and no email message issues. Go back and revise the form as necessary, and test again.

If the form works well but you receive no email message, check the following:

☆ Browser email preferences. Make sure a valid email return address and mail server are specified.

☆ Form Action: Make sure there are no spaces in the Form Action, and that your own email address is entered correctly. The Form Action should read something like `mailto:jlengel@bu.edu`

☆ Online status: make sure you have a live working connection to the Internet.

The form will eventually need to be tested from the Web server, with members of the target audience. This can wait until your entire site is posted to the Web server (as described in Chapter Seven), or it can be done before posting. You can send the page that contains the form to a tester by attaching it to an email and asking them to open it with their browser. If the form works correctly, you should soon receive an email message containing the form data from the tester.

Your Web site may need more than one form. It's best if no more than one form is put on the same page, but there's no problem including many forms on separate pages. Forms can help make sites interactive, even if they contain only a simple comment field, or a few survey buttons. Forms can help make the Web a two-way street—and Dreamweaver makes it easy to create these forms.

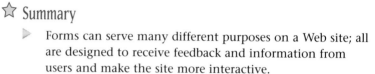

☆ Summary

▷ Forms can serve many different purposes on a Web site; all are designed to receive feedback and information from users and make the site more interactive.

▷ A form needs a clear purpose, a detailed list of the data to be collected, a determination of input types, and a clean, easy-to-use layout.

▷ The form action tells the browser where to send the contents of the form.

▷ Each type of form object is designed to collect a certain type of information, and to allow the user to make her choices easily and accurately.

▷ Before being published, a form should be tested in the browser by the developer, and again on the Web with typical users.

☆ Online References

Information on how to develop a form in Dreamweaver
`http://www.macromedia.com/support/dreamweaver/ts/documents/form_develop.htm`

An article, What the European Data Privacy Obligations Mean for U.S. Businesses
`http://www.gigalaw.com/articles/2001-all/harvey-2001-02-all.html`

☆ Review Questions

1. Describe at least five different functions that a form can accomplish in a Web site, and give an example of each one.

2. List the steps in the development of a Web form in Dreamweaver.

3. Explain the type of data that each of the following form objects is designed to collect: text field, text area, radio button, check box, popup menu.

4. Describe the process of setting up a series of radio buttons in Dreamweaver.

5. Under what conditions would a Web form require a layout table?

6. What preferences need to be set in the browser for an email form to work properly?

7. Can a form be tested in Dreamweaver? If not, how can it be tested?

☆ Hands-On Exercises

1. Browse the Web and find pages that use a form to accomplish each of the following functions: register for an event; collect audience feedback; enter information into a database; purchase a product; respond to a poll or survey; and enter search terms. Copy the URL of each example.

2. Design a form for your own Web site, including the following information: the purpose of the form; a list of each piece of data to be collected, with the label and the type of input for each; the instructions for the form; and a sketch of the layout.

3. Use Dreamweaver to insert a form and set its form action to send the contents to you as an email message.

4. Set up a layout table for your form, and insert at least one of each of these form objects: text field, text area, radio buttons, check boxes, popup menu, Submit button.

5. Set the email preferences of your browser as described in this chapter, and test your form in the browser. Then inspect the resulting email message for accuracy.

6. Test your form by posting it to a Web server or by emailing it to a tester, and examining the resulting email message for accuracy.

FORMATTING PAGES

 ## Draw the Lines

So far, you have been building simple and straightforward Web pages, without complex layout, design, or formatting. For many sites, this is sufficient, but an advanced site may require some page formatting. Just as many old-time boatbuilders can construct a simple craft "by eye," without plans or drawings, you can also build a Web site without formatting. But most bigger boats these days are built from a series of plans, called *lines*, which spell out exactly how each part will be built. This chapter shows how Dreamweaver lets you format the pages of your site using tables, templates, frames, and layers. You'll learn how to plan and implement the design of your site in each of these different methods.

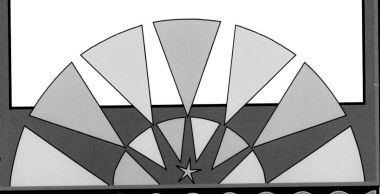

◎◉ Chapter Objectives

☆ To learn about the four different methods for formatting a Web page with Dreamweaver, and to know when each is appropriate

☆ To be able to format a page with a table, use the table to build a page, and extend the table format to the other pages of the site

☆ To learn how to create a Dreamweaver template with editable and repeating regions, and to use the template to build a page and a site

☆ To understand how frames work, and to be able to plan and build a site based on frames

☆ To understand how layers work in Dreamweaver, and to be able to plan and build a page based on layers

◎◉ Planning the Layout

The pages described in this book so far have used simple designs, with text and images aligned to the left or centered as in standard word-processing documents. But many Web pages need a more complex design—with columns and rows of information, menus running down the side or across the top, or all elements aligned on an invisible grid. In order to build a site like this, you must use one of the four layout methods provided by Dreamweaver:

☆ **Tables:** An HTML *table*, with *columns* and *rows*, organizes all of the elements of the page into its various *cells*.

☆ **Templates**: A *template* page with common *regions* serves as the basis of all the pages in the site. Templates often include tables.

☆ **Frames:** A *frameset* divides the page into separate *frames*, some of which change from page to page, and some of which remain constant.

☆ **Layers:** A blank page contains *layers* into which you insert the elements of the site.

The method you choose depends on the nature of the site that you are building, the capabilities of your users, and your willingness to deal with complexity in managing your site. *Tables* are the simplest method; *templates* are good for sites with many pages of identical layout; *frames* let you incorporate quick navigation; and *layers* let you place items anywhere on the page.

Same Layout, Different Methods

You can use any of these methods to lay out and build your page. In this chapter, we will build a Web page with identical content and appearance using each of the four methods. By doing this, you will learn the relative capabilities, limitations, and difficulties of each of the methods.

Figure 6.1 shows the home page for the Hog Island Yacht Club site formatted using tables. You can see the borders (not visible to the viewer) of a table with two rows and two columns.

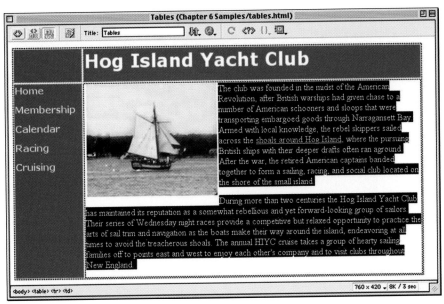

Figure 6.1 Page Formatted with a Table

Figure 6.2 shows the same page formatted using a template. You can see the two repeating template regions for the title and for the menu, and the editable region called *content*. These three regions are laid out in a table. As you create subsequent pages from this template, the repeating regions remain the same and the editable region is blank and ready for new input from page to page.

Figure 6.3 shows the page set up with three frames. The top right frame contains the title, which will be the same for all pages in the site, as will the left frame that contains the menu items. The large frame in the lower right contains the content that changes on every page. This method requires the development of four different HTML files: the *frameset* that defines the three frames, a page for the title, a page for the menu, and a page for the content.

Figure 6.4 shows the same page built with layers. The title, the menu, and the content each reside in their own layer.

Figure 6.2 Page Formatted with a Template

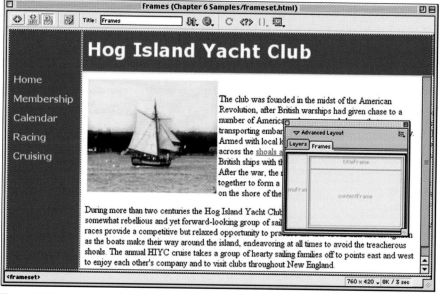

Figure 6.3 Page Built with Frames

Figure 6.4 Page Built with Layers

These pages appear slightly different in Dreamweaver, reflecting the particular methods used to build them. But in most recent browsers, they are virtually identical, and you would not be able to see the differences without looking at the HTML source code.

Pages can also be formatted in Dreamweaver with Cascading Style Sheets (CSS), but this is beyond the scope of this book. Information about this method of setting up a style sheet that is used in many pages can be found in the online references at the end of this chapter.

☆**WARNING** **No Guarantees**

No matter how carefully you plan and lay out your design or which method you use, you cannot guarantee that every user—regardless of browser, operating system, or display resolution—will see *exactly* the same thing. In general, the more complex your layout scheme is, the greater is the chance for differences among browsers. So keep your design simple, and test often with different browsers and resolutions.

Which Method Is Best?

The best method for you depends on the nature of your site, your own development capabilities, and the amount of work you are willing to put into the project. Tables are the easiest to create, and they work consistently across all browsers and platforms. But a template is more efficient than a table for creating a site with many identical pages, even though it takes some extra time to set up the template file. Frames require a frameset page as well as a separate page for each frame, and they need the developer's attention to create links and targets. This may be worth the trouble for some sites, since frames can create a consistent appearance and quicker development. Layers are quick and easy to set up, but may not work consistently across browsers and platforms, especially when the layers overlap.

For the beginning Web developer, it may be best to follow the order in this book: If you can format the site successfully with tables, use that method. If you need the efficiency of a template, go ahead and create one. If frames are appropriate for your site, you might next give that method a try. And save layers for last, because of the reasons cited above.

You will learn the most if you build your site in each of the four methods, in the order they are presented in this chapter. When you complete this process, you will better understand the differences between the methods and be able to make an educated choice about which method best meets your needs.

◎◎ Tables

Tables are the oldest and most reliable method for formatting a page, and the best choice for beginners' sites. Tables allow you set up the page in columns and rows, and to place items into the tables so they appear where you want them. Most commercial Web sites use tables to format their pages, and most beginners find it easy to understand and develop tables. In this method, you first sketch out the layout of your page, and then you insert a table on a new Dreamweaver document. Next, you adjust the table rows and columns to match your layout plan. Finally, you insert the various elements of your site into the appropriate cells of the table.

☆**TIP**   **Format Your Own Site**

The best way to use this chapter is to prepare the materials you need for a simple Web page as illustrated in the examples in this chapter—some text, an image, a title, and a set of menu items. Save these in a folder on your computer, and use them to build the same page in each of the four formats.

Sketch the Layout

With a pencil and paper, sketch the layout of your sample Web page. Show where the titles, menus, text, images, and other items will appear. You can see an example of such a sketch in Figure 3.2 on page 61.

In a lot of sites, the design you sketch will be used for many or all of the site's pages. Many Web designers mark off the sketch with some kind of layout grid that helps them align the various items on the page. The grid itself is invisible to the viewer, but essential to the developer, and may be used in the first three methods.

In the sketch, include the pixel dimensions of your page and its elements. You can learn more about sizing your page in *The Web Wizard's Guide to Web Site Design,* but for the purposes of this book, simply make sure that your page will be viewable comfortably by your audience—neither too small nor too large for their display screens and browser windows. Many developers design to a page size of 760 pixels wide and 420 pixels high, which is what a typical user with an 800 by 600 display will be able to see in her browser without scrolling.

☆ **SHORTCUT   Size the Window**

It's a good idea to set your Dreamweaver document window to the size of the browser window of your target audience. This is done by clicking the Window Size box in the lower right of the Dreamweaver Document window, and selecting one of the preset sizes.

Insert the Table

Sketch in hand, create a new Dreamweaver document by choosing File→New from the menubar and selecting Basic Page from the left column and HTML from the second. You will see a blank Dreamweaver document on your display, with the cursor blinking in the upper left corner.

☆ **SHORTCUT   Page Designs**

Dreamweaver provides you with pre-formatted table pages that you can select from the New Document dialog box. Take a look at some of these by selecting and creating them. Notice that they are all formatted with tables. But for your own work in this chapter, you will learn more if you build your own formatting from scratch.

To insert the formatting table, choose Insert→Table from the menubar. In the Insert Table dialog box, you will be able to enter the number of rows, the number of columns, and the width of your table.

To decide on these dimensions, you should consider your sketch. Make as many rows and columns as you need to implement your plan. In many cases, counting the gridlines on your sketch will help you determine the number of rows and columns.

You can set the width of the table either in pixels or as a percentage of the width of the browser's window. A table with a width set in pixels will always appear that wide, regardless of the size of the user's browser window or computer display. A table set as a percentage will stretch and shrink to fit the size of the user's browser. The table set in pixels will be more consistent in appearance, but may not fill the screen properly, while the table set as a percentage will always fill the screen, but may not look the same for all viewers—text and images may shift position to fit the window size.

The Web page shown in Figure 6.1 was built on a table of two rows and two columns, set to a width of 100% with a border width of zero. Your page may need a different set of table parameters, depending on its design.

When you insert the table, it will appear as a set of dotted lines, as shown in Figure 6.5.

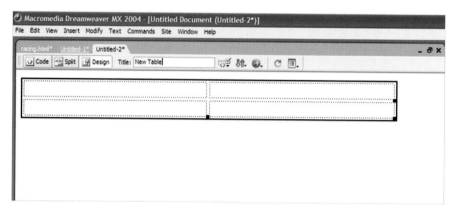

Figure 6.5 New Table on Page

You can stretch this table down to the bottom of the page, and then adjust its dividing lines to match your sketch by clicking and dragging the mouse. The adjusted table for the page shown in Figure 6.1 is shown in Figure 6.6. Adjust your table to match the grid in your sketch.

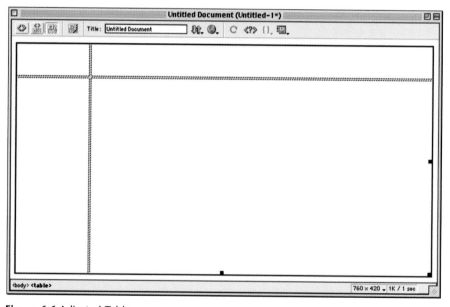

Figure 6.6 Adjusted Table

This adjusted table becomes the basis for the format of your page. Save your work so far, following the rules for Web filenames and folder organization covered in Chapter One.

Insert the Content

You will insert the content of your page into the cells of this table. For the example shown in Figure 6.1, we typed the title into the top right cell of the table and the menu items into the left cell. We inserted the image of the boat into the lower right cell, aligned it to the left, and then typed or pasted the body text. At this point, the page looks like Figure 6.7.

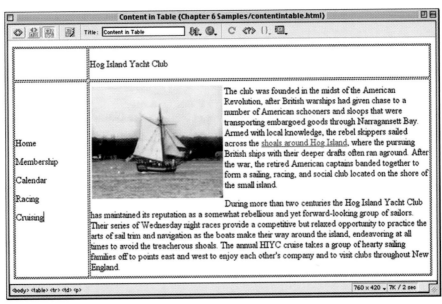

Figure 6.7 Inserting Content into Table

Insert the content of your sample page into the cells of the table. You may find that some items may stretch the cells when they are inserted, and you may need to drag the dividers back to their desired positions.

Adjust the Format

Once the content is in the table, you can adjust it and the parameters of the cells to achieve your desired design result.

☆ *Text:* Following the instructions in Chapter One, set the size, font, color, alignment, and style of the text as appropriate.

☆ *Alignment:* Align the content within the cell by using the Properties window as shown in Figure 6.8. (The Dreamweaver default setting aligns the content vertically in the *middle* of the cell, and often must be changed to align to the *top* of the cell.)

☆ *Cell background color:* Set the cell background color in the Properties window as shown in Figure 6.8. This is done by clicking in the cell, then clicking the box labeled Bg color, and finally clicking the desired color.

Figure 6.8 Adjusting Text and Cell Properties

☆**WARNING** **Text Color and Background Color**

If you set the color of your text to be the same color as the cell background, you won't see the words on the screen. In the example shown in this chapter, the white text in the title was temporarily invisible until the cell's background color was set to red.

Adjust the content and the cell color in your site to meet the requirements of your design. You may want to try out several possibilities for size, color, and alignment to find the one that works best. Preview your page often in the browser to see exactly what it will look like to the viewer (which may be different from what you see in the Dreamweaver document window).

☆**TIP** **Adjust Groups of Cells**

You can select several cells of a table at once, and adjust them with one click. Use ⎡Shift⎤+click to select the cells, and then adjust the necessary items in the Properties window; this change will be applied to all the cells.

Save the Table Page

Save your page often as you work. Save one version with all the content, and save another version—with a different filename—that contains only the content that will be shared by many pages. In the example shown in this chapter, we cleared out the content in the lower right cell and saved the page (with the title and menu cells full) with the filename *master.html*. This page can be used as the formatted basis of additional pages in the same site: Open the *master.html* page, fill in the lower right cell, choose Save As from the file menu, and then save page under a new name.

☆**TIP** **Set Up the Menu Links**

Many Web sites include a common set of menu items that appear on every page, as in the example shown above. If you set up a formatting table and save it for later use to build additional pages, it's a good idea to build the links for the menu items into the common page at the beginning. In this way, you only need to make the links once, and they will work for the entire site.

Merging and Splitting Cells

Your formatting may work better if you can split and join the cells of your formatting table. This can provide the flexibility you need to make items appear just where you want them. To combine two cells into one, select them both by shift-clicking, and then choose Modify→Table→Merge Cells. To split a cell into two rows or columns, select the cell, and then choose Modify→Table→Split Cell from the menubar.

☆ **SHORTCUT** **Use the Properties Window**

The manipulation of cells in a table or of text on a page may be more easily accomplished in the Properties window than with menus. Select the item you want to change, and then click the appropriate button or box in the Properties window. If you know the keyboard shortcuts for working with text, you may find those useful also as you format your words.

About Formatting Tables

A good way to learn how tables are used to format a page is examine the tables in a commercial Web site. Let's look at a couple of Web sites.

Connect to a site that is formatted with tables, such as `http://www.nytimes.com/`. Wait until the page loads fully, and then choose File→Save As from the menubar. Save the page to your computer as HTML source. Open this file with Dreamweaver. You will not see the images or much of the text, but you will see the outlines of the tables that the *Times* developers used to format their page. Theirs is a complex design that requires tables within tables. Click on each table and see how it is formatted by studying its Properties window.

A simpler table-formatted page can be found at `http://www.bristolri.com/`. In this example, you can see the tables aligned next to each other left to right across the page.

You can be sure that the developers of these sites have tweaked the size, alignment, and other attributes of these tables many times to get them to format the page so that it appears as they desire. While your site may not be as complex as these, it will nonetheless probably need considerable adjustment until it works just right.

◎◎ Templates

Using a template to format your Web site takes the concept of the table one step further. A template is a special kind of file in a Web site that provides the common elements for a collection of similarly formatted pages in the site. You can develop the template once and easily build the rest of the pages based on it. And if you need to change one of the common elements by adding or deleting a menu item, you only need to change it once on the template page, and it will change on every page made from that template.

Building a template page involves the same sketching, gridding, and table-making described above in the section on tables. In fact, a template page is almost always built on a table. To build a template page, first go through the steps of building a table-formatted page, up until just before you insert the content.

> ☆ **WARNING**   Define Your Site
>
> In order to use templates, you must first go through Dreamweaver's site definition process. To do this, choose Site→New Site from the menubar, enter a name for your site, and then set the local root folder to be your Web site folder. You'll find more information about defining a site in Chapter Seven.

Plan Your Regions

A template page contains some *repeating regions*, some *editable regions*, and perhaps some *optional regions*. Repeating regions appear in the same place with the same content on every page. Editable regions are different on every page. Optional regions may appear on some pages, but not others. In the example shown in Figure 6.2, the title and the menus are placed in repeating regions, and the picture and body text appear in an editable region.

On your sketch, indicate which items will be in the various regions, and assign a name to each region. Items such as site titles, site menus, copyright information, and organizational logos that appear consistently across the site should be in repeating regions. Content that appears on only one page should be in an editable region. Items that appear on many, but not all pages can be placed in an optional region.

Create a New Template Page

To build a template from scratch, choose File→New from the menubar, select Template Page from the left column and HTML Template from the right column, and then click the Create button in the lower right. You will see a Dreamweaver document window with << Template >> in the titlebar. Into this page insert a table and set it up to format your page, as you did earlier.

Save this template with a proper filename and the filename extension .dwt into your Web site folder.

Insert Regions

It's best to insert the repeating regions first, and then work on the editable regions. To insert a repeating region, first click in the cell of the table where you want it to appear. Then choose Insert→Template Objects→Repeating Region from the menubar. Enter a name for this region. Leave the content alone for now. In the same manner, you can create additional repeating regions, optional regions, and editable regions on your template.

Align these regions in the cells of your table. At this point, your template may look like Figure 6.9.

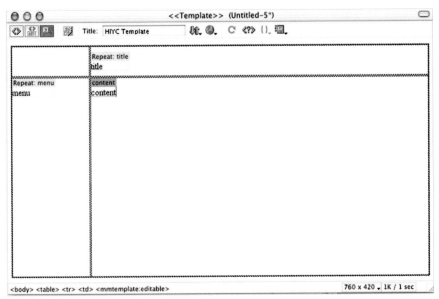

Figure 6.9 Inserting Regions in a Template

If your table needs background colors in some of its cells, set those now, as described in the previous section on tables.

Edit Repeating Regions

Enter the text or insert the images that go in each of your repeating regions—the items that appear the same on every page made with the template. To do this, place the cursor in the region, and then type or paste the text or insert the image. Format the size, style, color, alignment, and font of the text as necessary. Also, size and align the image as necessary. The formatting you apply to the contents of these regions will appear automatically on all pages that use this template.

Insert the content for any optional regions in this template, and format it as necessary. Do not put any content into the editable regions. You will do this later, when you create individual pages from this template.

Save the Template

Once the template looks the way you want and the repeating and optional regions are filled, it's time to save the template. Save your template to the *templates* folder in your Web folder; Dreamweaver should automatically select this for you. Assign a proper Web filename, and Dreamweaver will add its special .dwt filename extension. You will use this template to build additional pages for your site. You may now close the template file.

Build Pages from the Template

To build pages that are based on the template you just saved, follow these steps:

1. Choose File→New... from the menubar.

2. Click the Templates tab at the top of the New Document dialog box, as shown in Figure 6.10.

3. Choose your site from the left column, and the template from the right column.

4. Click the Create button in the lower right to open the template.

5. Insert text, images, or other content into the editable regions of this document.

6. Save the completed page with its own filename into your Web folder.

Additional pages for your site can be built from this template by repeating these steps.

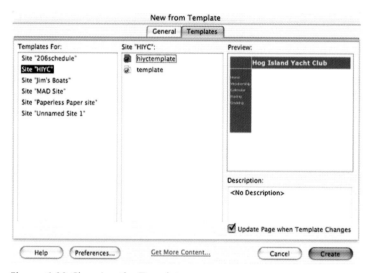

Figure 6.10 Choosing the Template

To change items in the repeating regions, you will need to open the template (.dwt) file directly and resave it with the changes. These changes will be reflected in all the pages that were built from this template. To change items in the editable regions, you will need to open each page directly, make the changes, and save the page.

Frames

Formatting a site with frames is more complex than the other methods, and requires some planning up front. A frames site begins with a *frameset*, a special kind of Web page that has no content at all—it simply sets up a collection of *frames* into which other Web pages will be displayed in a browser. The Web page shown in Figure 6.3, for instance, has a frameset with three frames, one for the title, one for the menu, and one for the content. The frame window for this page is shown in Figure 6.11.

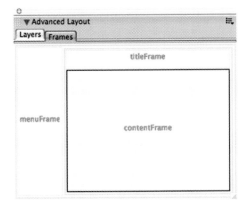

Figure 6.11 Sample Frame Window

For each frame, the frameset tells the browser which Web page to display. In this example, the titleframe will display the page *title.html*, the menuframe will display the file *menu.html*, and the contentframe will display the page *welcome.html*. When the browser opens this frameset, it looks for the three pages and places them in the proper frames. Thus four documents are needed to display this page: the frameset and the three component pages that show in the three frames.

As a user navigates through a Web site built with frames, some frames remain constant, while others change. In the site shown in Figure 6.3, for instance, the menu frame never changes. Nor does the title frame. Only the content frame changes. So when you click the menu item Racing, the page *racing.html* is placed into the content frame, but all else remains the same. The frameset does not reload, nor do the menu and title pages.

To build a site with frames, you first plan the frameset and design the various pages that will go into it. You also plan the names of each frame and the filename of each page. Then you create the frameset and name and organize the frames. Next you create the component pages, and test the results in the browser.

Frames

Plan the Frameset

The planning that you did for the tables and template page may serve as the basis for your frameset. Your frameset should be laid out in rectangles, with some areas that remain constant while others change. For your first frameset, use no more than two or three frames. Consider a title frame, a menu frame, and a content frame, as in the examples shown earlier in this chapter.

Sketch your frameset on paper. Give each frame a name, and also make a note of the content that will appear in each frame. Select a filename for each of the component pages that will go into the frames.

☆ **TIP**   **Fill the Page**

The frames that you plan must fill the page—you can't leave any blank areas. Use horizontal and vertical lines to divide the page into a set of frames that fill the page.

Create the Frameset

Create your frameset by choosing File→New... from the menubar. Then choose Framesets from the left column and one of the sample sets from the right column of the New Document dialog box, as shown in Figure 6.12.

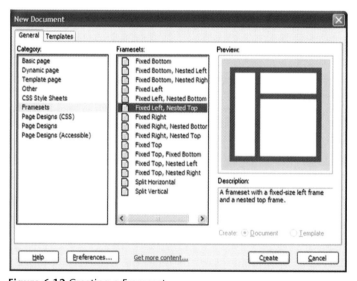

Figure 6.12 Creating a Frameset

This will open a new Dreamweaver document with the frames you selected. Open the Frames window by choosing Window→Others→Frames from the menubar. In the Frames window you will see a miniature duplicate of the frameset.

Name the Frames

Each frame should have a name that makes sense, since you will need to refer to it when you manage your links and targets a little further on. To name a frame, select it in the small Frames window (not in the big Document window), and then in the Properties window enter a name. Keep the name short and descriptive, with no spaces or special characters, as shown in Figure 6.13.

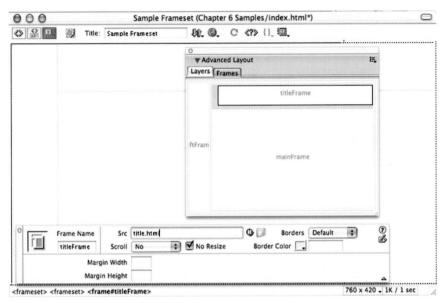

Figure 6.13 Naming a Frame

While you are working in the Frame Properties window, set the source file for this frame—the name of the Web page file that will be displayed in this frame, as shown in Figure 6.13. Set the names and sources for all of the frames in your frameset.

Save the Frameset

Choose File→Save Frameset from the menubar. Enter a name for the frameset. In many cases, this frameset will serve as your home or index page—the page that the server sends whenever a viewer makes a connection to your site. If that's the case, enter *index.html* as the name of the frameset, and save it into your Web folder.

The purpose of a frameset is simply to set the size and location of the frames, and to tell the browser which file to display in each frame. The HTML code for a simple frameset might look like this:

```
<frameset rows="*" cols="128,*" frameborder="NO" border="0"
        framespacing="0">
  <frame src="menu.html" name="menuFrame" scrolling="NO"
        noresize id="menuFrame">
```

```
<frameset rows="69,*" cols="*" framespacing="0"
    frameborder="NO" border="0">
  <frame src="title.html" name="titleFrame"
      scrolling="NO" noresize id="titleFrame">
  <frame src="welcome.html" name="contentFrame"
      id="contentFrame">
</frameset>
</frameset>
```

The code tells the browser to

⭐ Make a frameset of as many rows as necessary, 128 pixels wide, with no border or spacing;

⭐ Place into this frameset a frame that displays the file *menu.html*, is called *menuFrame*, and cannot be scrolled or resized;

⭐ Place into this frameset another frameset 69 pixels high and as wide as necessary, with no spacing or border;

⭐ Place two frames into this second frameset—one for the title (*title.html*) and a second for the content (*welcome.html*).

That's all there is to the frameset—a set of directions for setting up the frames and pointing to the files that will be displayed in them.

Create the Component Pages

Use Dreamweaver to create standard Web pages for each of the component files of your frameset. Consider the size of the frames as you create the component pages. It's a good idea to set the window size of the Dreamweaver document to the size of the frame as you are building the content of the component pages, so you will be sure that it will fit.

Save each component page with the filename listed in the frameset, and save it in the same folder as the frameset file.

> ⭐ **SHORTCUT Work Right in the Frames**
>
> Dreamweaver lets you create the component pages right in the frameset Document window. Just click in one of the frames in the big Document window (not the little Frames window), and insert the content as usual. When you are done with each frame, choose File→Save Frame As... from the menubar and save each frame with the filename you assigned in the frameset.

You will need more component pages than you have frames in the frameset. At lease one of the frames will take on many different pages as the user navigates the site. In the example shown in Figure 6.3, there are five different pages that may appear in the content frame, one for each menu item. Create at least three different component pages for at least one of the frames in your frameset.

When all your components are complete, preview the frameset in the browser. Don't worry if the page does not appear exactly as you planned—you'll learn soon how to adjust the frames to format the page exactly as necessary. But first you need to make the frames work for navigation.

Manage Links and Targets

The operation of a frameset relies on links with *targets*. For instance, when the user clicks the menu item *Racing* in the example shown in Figure 6.3, the page *racing.html* appears in the content frame. The word *racing* in the *menu.html* page is linked to the *racing.html* page, with its target frame set to *contentFrame*. The target of the link is the name of the frame in which it is to appear. By using targets, you can allow a click in one frame to change the contents of another.

On a Web site, if no frame is targeted, each link opens in the same browser window as the sending page; the new (link to) page replaces the old (link from) page. When a target is added to a link, the new page can be made to open in a different frame or window, leaving the sending page where it was.

To create links and targets to make your frameset work, follow these steps:

1. Open your menu page in Dreamweaver, or click in the menu frame in your frameset Document window.

2. Select the text or image that you want to make into a link.

3. In the Properties window, enter or browse to the page you want to link to, as shown in Figure 6.14.

4. Also in the Properties window, enter or choose from the popup menu the name of the frame you want as the target for this link, as shown in Figure 6.14.

5. Test the operation of the link by previewing the frameset in the browser.

Figure 6.14 Making Links with Targets

Do the same for all of your menu items, or at least those for which you created component pages. Test the operation of the frameset by previewing it in the browser.

☆ **TIP**   **Targets**

When you are creating a link in a frames page, the Properties window shows in its list of possible targets _blank, _parent, _self, and _top, as well as all of the frames in the frameset. A _blank target opens the link in a new browser window. A _parent target causes the linked page to replace the entire frameset. A _self target opens in the frame you are working from, and a _top target opens in the topmost window on the display.

Adjust the Frames

Your frameset may operate well, but it may not look right. In most cases you will need to make some adjustments to the frame sizes, borders, and scrolling properties. Here's how.

1. Open your frameset document in Dreamweaver.

2. Open the Frames window by choosing Window➔Others➔Frames from the menubar.

3. Open the Properties window by choosing Window➔Properties from the menubar.

4. Click the frame you want to adjust in the Frames window.

In the Properties window, you can adjust several attributes of this frame:

☆ Whether it *scrolls* always, automatically as necessary, or not at all.

☆ The thickness and color of its *border*.

☆ The height and width of its *margins*.

Set these to fit the needs of your design.

To change the size of a frame, click the frame border in the little Frames window. Then in the Properties window, enter the size of the frame in the box labeled Row or Column, as shown in Figure 6.15.

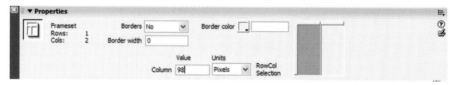

Figure 6.15 Adjusting Frame Size

You may find that you need to preview the frameset in the browser, test its appearance and operation, and make adjustments in several cycles before you are finished.

(margin: Frames)

☆**TIP**   **Links and Targets**

A common problem with sites formatted with frames is the appearance of a component page in the wrong frame. You may see, for instance, one of your content pages replacing the items in the menu frame. The cause of this is a faulty target in the link from the menu item. Check all your links to make sure they show the correct target frame in the Properties window.

◎◎ Layers

While the sample page we have been working with may be formatted using the layers method, as shown in Figure 6.4, this may not be the best choice. Layers are best used for relatively simple designs in which the items on the page are not in columns and rows, but scattered around the page in something other than a rectilinear pattern. Figure 6.16 shows the kind of page that might best be formatted with layers, rather than with the more reliable methods described above.

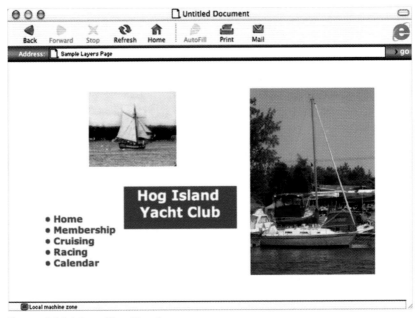

Figure 6.16 A Page That Uses Layers

Plan the Page

When planning a page to be formatted with layers, you need not set up a grid as with the other methods. Instead, sketch the items on the page wherever you wish to see them. Keep the items from overlapping, since overlapping layers do not work consistently. A single layer may contain text, images, multimedia, or a combination of items, but it may be easier for you to restrict each layer to just one item.

Insert the Layers

To insert a layer, choose Insert→Layer from the menubar. A layer will appear on the page as a rectangle with a square over its upper left corner, as shown in Figure 6.17.

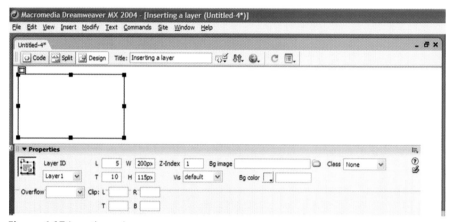

Figure 6.17 Inserting a Layer

The layer's Properties window shows:

☆ Its *location* on the page, indicated in the boxes labeled L (left) and T (top), meaning that the top left corner of this layer is located at a point 5 pixels over from the left edge of the page, and 10 pixels down from the top.

☆ Its *size*, indicated in the boxes labeled W (width)—200, and H (height)—115, in pixels.

☆ Its background color or image, if any.

Clicking on the edge of the layer shows its handles, which you can drag to change its size. Clicking and dragging the edge of the layer with the hand allows you to move it around inside the Dreamweaver Document window.

Insert the layers you need to execute your plan, and drag them to the desired locations on the page.

Insert Data

You can insert items into a layer just as you insert them onto a regular document. Click inside the layer, and then type the text, or choose Insert→Image from the menubar. The layer will grow to accommodate the content that you insert into it. A layer can also contain animations, movies, sounds, or other types of media. Insert the content you need in each layer. You can continue to resize the layers and move them around the page as you insert the content. Just be careful not to overlap the layers. Choose Window→Others→Layers, and check the Prevent Overlaps box to make sure there is no overlapping.

Preview the Page

To ensure that the layers are working well, preview the page often in the browser. With layers, it's a good idea to preview in several browsers, since each browser interprets layers a bit differently.

If your layers are not appearing correctly, you may get better results by letting Dreamweaver convert the layers formatting to the more reliable tables method. Choose Modify→Convert→Layers to tables from the menubar, and then save the converted page.

Layers

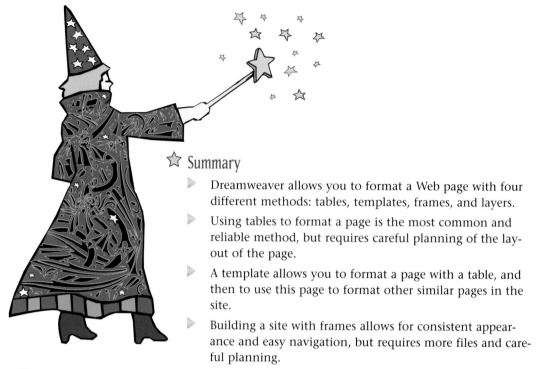

☆ Summary

▷ Dreamweaver allows you to format a Web page with four different methods: tables, templates, frames, and layers.

▷ Using tables to format a page is the most common and reliable method, but requires careful planning of the layout of the page.

▷ A template allows you to format a page with a table, and then to use this page to format other similar pages in the site.

▷ Building a site with frames allows for consistent appearance and easy navigation, but requires more files and careful planning.

▷ Formatting with layers allows the most freedom of design but is most reliable with simple pages.

☆ Online References

Using cascading style sheets in Dreamweaver
`http://www.macromedia.com/support/dreamweaver/layout/css/`

Page layout with Dreamweaver
`http://www.macromedia.com/support/dreamweaver/layout.html`

Using tables to present content
`http://www.macromedia.com/support/dreamweaver/pages_tables.html`

Which to use—frames or tables?
`http://www.macromedia.com/support/dreamweaver/layout/frames_or_tables/`

Web design with Dreamweaver templates
`http://www.macromedia.com/devnet/mx/dreamweaver/articles/dw_templates.html`

☆ Review Questions

1. Describe four different ways to format a Web page with Dreamweaver.
2. Explain the kinds of pages that are best built with each of the four methods of formatting.
3. List the steps involved in planning the formatting of a Web page.
4. List an advantage and a disadvantage of each of the four methods of formatting pages.

5. Describe the process of formatting a page with tables.

6. What are the three types of regions in a Dreamweaver template page, and what is each used for?

7. What is the relationship between the frameset page and the component pages in a site formatted with frames?

8. What type of formatting is best done with layers in Dreamweaver?

☆ Hands-On Exercises

1. Develop a sketch of your Web site format, using a grid system and showing the content for each part of the page.

2. Execute your sketch using tables in Dreamweaver. Develop at least four pages that use the same formatting.

3. Turn your tables design into a Dreamweaver template, and from this template develop at least four pages for your Web site.

4. Find a commercial Web site that is built with frames, and examine the frameset by downloading the page and opening it with Dreamweaver. Open each of the component pages as well.

5. Develop your own sample site using frames. Include at least three component pages, and at least three links with targets.

6. Develop your own sample Web page using layers in Dreamweaver. Test this page on at least two browsers on two platforms.

WEB SITE MANAGEMENT

Organize the Fleet

S o far this book has concentrated on building individual Web pages with Dreamweaver; using its features to include text, images, and multimedia; and formatting all of these into a workable layout. This chapter looks at the management of an entire Web site, which is made up of many pages and multiple media files. If each separate Web page is a boat that you have assembled, a complete Web site is like a fleet of ships, organized and coordinated to accomplish their mission.

Chapter Objectives

☆ To learn the essential steps in planning a Web site and creating a flow chart for the site

☆ To be able properly to organize materials for the site into folders

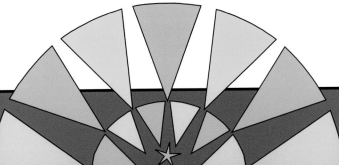

☆ To learn how to use Dreamweaver's site definition and management tools, including a site map and file list

☆ To understand how to use Dreamweaver to publish a Web site to a remote Web server

☆ To be able to manage a site, both locally and remotely, using Dreamweaver's built-in tools

◎◎ Planning a Web Site

The key to successful Web site management is careful planning at the very beginning. You will find a more thorough treatment of site planning in *The Web Wizard's Guide to Web Design*, but the basic process will be covered here. Good planning requires that you first identify the audience and purpose of your site, outline its content, and draw a flow chart of its structure. In many cases, it's also important to sketch out the design of your site, as mentioned in Chapter Six. All this planning should be done before you even launch Dreamweaver—it will make the job of managing the site much easier.

Identify the Audience and Purpose

Who is going to look at your Web site? What will it do for them? The answers to these two questions will guide your work as a Web author. Your first task is to spell out, in writing, the audience and purpose of your site.

Picture the folks who will be visiting your site. Who are they? Why are they there? What kind of people are they? How are they connected to the Internet? For the Hog Island Yacht Club site we have used as an example in this book, our audience is twofold:

☆ Members of the HIYC who visit the site to get information and sign up for events.

☆ Potential members and visitors who want to find out what the club has to offer.

Since individuals in both of these groups are likely to be more interested in boats than in computers, we cannot expect them to own the very latest high-powered computers, nor can we count on many of them enjoying high-speed connections to the Internet. But we can expect them to be wealthy enough to own a boat, and to live in the geographical area surrounding Hog Island. Most will be between 22 and 72 years of age, based on the age distribution of the current membership. This knowledge will help us build a site that fits their particular needs.

This audience will want to know the club rules and regulations, get information and sign up for club events (especially races and cruises), and learn how to become a member.

Planning a Web Site

> ☆**TIP**   **Web Design Book**
>
> Chapter Two of *The Web Wizard's Guide to Web Design* presents a detailed process for identifying the audience and purpose of a Web site. Consult that book for more information on how to prepare your own planning documents.

For your own site, set forth a similar definition of its audience and purpose. This will make outlining the content and charting the structure of your site much easier.

Outline the Content

Review what you wrote about the purpose of your Web site. From this list of purposes, you should be able to generate an outline of the site's contents. The contents of our HIYC site might look like this:

☆ Summary of HIYC history and mission

☆ HIYC rules and regulations

☆ Calendar of HIYC events

☆ Information and sign-up for Wednesday night races

☆ Information and sign-up for HIYC cruises

☆ Information for potential members

  • How to join

  • Online application form

☆ Reports of past HIYC events (with video and pictures)

In this list of contents, you should be able to find materials for each of the purposes set forth earlier. When you write your own content outline, review your purposes and make sure there's something in the outline for each one. If you are working with a team or a client, run the audience, purpose, and content outline of the site by them, and get their suggestions and approval before going on to the next steps.

Draw a Flow Chart

A flow chart is graphic representation of the structure of the Web site. It's essential to good site development and management. The flow chart is built from the content outline, and contains planning information that guides the rest of the management work.

The flow chart for the HIYC Web site might look like Figure 7.1.

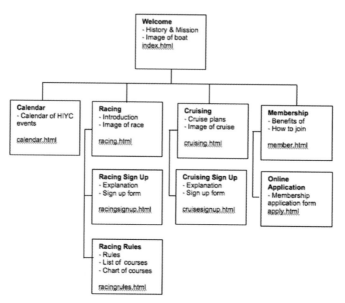

Figure 7.1 Flow Chart for HIYC Web Site

Each rectangle on the chart represents a Web page, and contains the title, contents, and filename of the page. The connecting lines show the links between the pages. This chart was constructed with Microsoft Word, using text boxes for the pages and the drawing toolbar for the lines. A useful flow chart can also be created with pencil and paper, or with specialized charting software. The important elements are:

☆ The definition of each page in the site as a rectangle

☆ The specification of the contents of each page

☆ The filename of each page

☆ The lines that show the links between the pages

Before working further in this chapter, draw a flow chart for your own site, providing all of the essential information. When you are done, review again your statement of purpose, as well as the outline of contents, and make sure all of the site's goals are covered in the flow chart. You'll refer to this flow chart throughout the site management process.

Sketch the Design

In many Web sites, pages share a common design. As part of the planning process, sketch this design (or several designs if necessary to accommodate different types of pages in the site). Set forth colors, fonts, sizes, common elements, and other aspects of the overall design. More information on completing this task can be found in Chapter Two of *The Web Wizard's Guide to Web Design*.

You should include in your sketch any tables, frames, templates, or layers that you plan to use. Refer to Chapter Six of this book as you sketch the design. If you are using frames, the design should also include the names of the frames in the frameset and the filenames of the component pages, as described in Chapter Six.

Organizing the Site

With your planning accomplished, you are ready to organize the site on your computer and gather its elements. The site that you will build and save on your own computer is called the *local site*, and it is essential that this site be set up properly at the outset to work well with Dreamweaver's site management tools.

Setting up Folders

A Web site is best built inside a single folder (or directory) on your computer's hard disk. This folder will later be copied to a Web server when you publish the site, so it's important that the folder be set up properly. Your site folder should have a short, simple filename that will work well on the Web, one with no spaces, no punctuation, no capital letters, and no special characters. For our sample site, a good folder name might be *hiyc*. Poor choices would include *HIYC Web Site*, *hiyc.web*, and *HIYC/website*.

Inside the site folder will go all of the files that make up your site: HTML pages, image files, media files, and template files. For simple sites with fewer than a dozen pages, all of the elements can be saved directly into the site folder, without the need for subfolders. But for a more complex site with dozens or hundreds of files, you will find it easier to manage if you create subfolders. A subfolder called *images* might contain all the pictures, and another called *media* might contain the animations, sounds, and videos, for example. Dreamweaver will automatically create a *templates* subfolder inside your site to contain any Dreamweaver templates that you create.

If our HIYC site were complex enough to warrant it, the folder organization at this stage might look like Figure 7.2.

Figure 7.2 Folders for HIYC Site

Set up the folders you need for your own site on the hard disk of your computer or on other media that you will use to store your local site.

Gathering the Elements

Dreamweaver does not automatically put the files that make up your site into those folders; you have to put them there yourself. In most cases, you will gather the media elements first—the images, sounds, videos, and animations—and save them into the Web site folder. As you prepare these files, refer to the advice in the early chapters of this book about each type of media.

☆ For advice on preparing image files, see Chapter Three.

☆ For advice on preparing animation, sound, and video files, see Chapter Four.

Make sure each file is saved in the proper format, with a filename that will work on the Web. Be sure each filename ends with the proper three-letter filename extension, as described in Chapters Three and Four. For a small site, save all the files into your Web site folder. For more complex sites, save them in the images or media subfolders as appropriate.

After the elements have been gathered and saved into the Web site folder, you can build your pages as described in Chapters One through Six of this book, inserting elements as appropriate onto the pages. Dreamweaver will remember where the elements came from, and embed their filename and location into the HTML code of the page. The HTML pages, of course, must also be saved to the Web site folder.

☆**WARNING** **Don't Lose the Elements**

When you insert an image, sound, video, or animation into a Dreamweaver document, the item does not get drawn into the Dreamweaver document. It remains separate, and Dreamweaver retrieves it from the Web site folder every time you open the document. And when you save a Dreamweaver document, the elements are not saved with it—only the HTML code is saved. So keep those image and media files in your folder—your site won't work without them.

◎◎ Defining the Site

Once the folders are set up and the elements gathered, you are ready to let Dreamweaver *define* your site. A site definition is Dreamweaver's way of keeping track of all the files that make up your site. You don't need a site definition to create a simple site, but you do need one if you want to use Dreamweaver to publish your site to a Web server, or if you want to take advantage of Dreamweaver's site management tools.

You can define a site at the outset, before it is built, as we are describing here, or you can define an already existing site. This chapter provides instructions for both methods.

Define Your Site

At this point in the development process, you should define your local site, the one you're building on your own computer. (In the next section of this chapter you will define the remote site, the one that's on the Web server.) From Dreamweaver's menu bar, choose Site→New Site. Choose this menu item even if you want to define an already existing site. In the Site Definition dialog box, as shown in Figure 7.3, you will provide the information necessary to define your site.

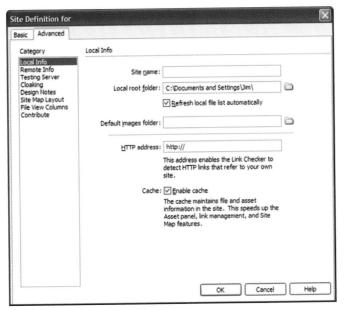

Figure 7.3 Site Definition Dialog Box

Follow these steps to define the local copy of your site:

1. Choose Site→New Site from the menubar.

2. Click the Advanced tab at the top of the Site Definition dialog box. (The Basic tab takes you through a site definition wizard, which you can also use, but the Advanced tab is more useful.)

3. Enter a name for your site in the box labeled Site Name. This name is only for your reference while you are developing the site; the audience will not see it. This need not be the name of your site folder.

4. Choose your Local Root Folder by clicking the folder icon to the right of the box, and then navigating to your Web site folder.

5. If you have created a separate folder for your site's images, choose it as the Default Images Folder.

   In the left column, click Site Map Layout

6. Select your site's home page by clicking the folder icon to the right of the box and then navigating to your site's home page.

7. Click OK.

This will bring up a Site dialog box that shows a list of your site's files on the right, as shown in Figure 7.4. Make sure this is the correct list of files and folders for your site.

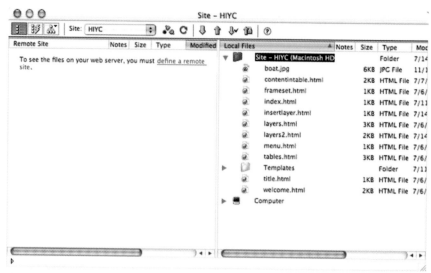

Figure 7.4 Site File List

You will use this dialog box to help you manage your site as you build and publish it. The buttons along the top and the items under the Site menu let you organize your files, publish files to the Web server, and edit the site in a variety of ways, as you will learn later in this chapter.

☆ **SHORTCUT**   **Selecting the Home Page**

In most cases, the home page will have the filename *index.html*. That's because most Web servers are set up to send the *index.html* file automatically when a user connects to the site. Select the site's home page by choosing Site→Site Map View→Set As Home Page from the menubar. You must select the home page in order to view the Site Map.

Site Map

Figure 7.4 shows the site as a list of files. You can also view a Site Map, as shown in Figure 7.5.

To see the Site Map View, click the Site Map button at the upper left of the Site dialog box, or choose View→Site Map from the menubar. The site map shows the pages, and the links between them, in a manner similar to your flow chart. You can double-click a page in the map to edit it. Many developers find the site map the easiest view to work with.

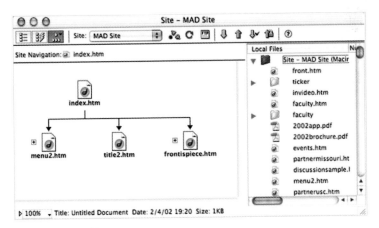

Figure 7.5 Site Map

◎◎ Publishing the Site

Once your site is built locally on your computer, and you have tested it by previewing it in the browser so that you know it works, it's time to publish the site on the World Wide Web. Dreamweaver refers to the copy of the site on the Web server as the *remote site*. To do this, you need a functioning local site, fully defined as described above. You also need access to a Web server. You can use Dreamweaver to send your site to the server, and to manage the updating and coordination of both the local and remote sites.

Web Servers

Web servers are computers that are

☆ Connected permanently to the Internet

☆ Running 24 hours a day, 365 days a year

☆ Running software that receives requests for Web pages and serves them to the audience

While any computer can be set up to act as a Web server, in most cases an organization will dedicate a computer to this purpose, ensure its continual operation and maintenance, and control access to its disk drives. Most organizations, including schools, colleges, and businesses, designate a Webmaster to configure and manage the Web server and its software. And many Internet service providers let you use their Web server as part of your account.

For your site to be accessible by its audience over the Web, it must reside on a Web server. To get your site onto the server, you must work with the Webmaster, or the person who manages your organization's Web server. In a few cases, the Webmaster may ask you to deliver the completed site to her on a CD-ROM or other medium, and she will copy it to the server for you. But in most cases, the Webmaster or Internet service provider will give you a username and password that will allow you to copy the site to the server yourself, over the Internet. Dreamweaver is ready to help you to do this. In most organizations, you will copy the site to the remote server using one of two methods:

☆ Using the Internet's File Transfer Protocol (FTP)

☆ Using your Local Area Network (LAN)

The Webmaster will advise you on which method to use.

Publishing with FTP

This method of copying your site to the server is most often used when the Web server is located at a distance, and not on your Local Area Network. To use the FTP method with Dreamweaver, you will need to know three things:

☆ The *host name* of the Web server. This is the unique name that distinguishes it from all other computers connected to the Internet. Host names are most often in the form *webdev.bu.edu*, but may sometimes be listed as an IP address such as *128.197.190.178*. The Webmaster will let you know the host name of the Web server you will be using.

☆ Your *username* on the server. Only authorized users may copy files to the Web server, so access to it is protected by a username and password system. The Webmaster will provide you with an FTP username for the Web server.

☆ Your *password*. This also comes from the Webmaster, and allows you to access the Web server to copy files.

Once you've acquired these three pieces of information, you are ready to use Dreamweaver to define your remote site using FTP access.

Publishing Over the LAN

When the Web server is located on your organization's Local Area Network, it may be easier to use this method to publish your site. You will need to find out three things from the Webmaster to make this work:

☆ The *pathname* to the Web server. This consists of a string of characters that describes the location of the Web directory on the LAN. It may look something like *COM01/web/students/*.

☆ Your *username* for the server. As with FTP, access over the LAN to the Web server is also controlled.

☆ Your *password* for the server. This plus your username lets you connect to the server over the LAN so you may copy your site.

Once you have this information, you are ready to define your remote site.

Defining the Remote Site

In Dreamweaver, open your Site window by choosing Site→Edit Sites from the menubar. Select your site—the one you defined earlier—and click the Edit button. In the Site Definition dialog box, select Remote Info from the Category list on the left, as shown in Figure 7.6.

From the Access popup menu, choose *FTP* or *Local Network*, according to the advice of your Webmaster. Choosing FTP will display text boxes for you to enter the Web server host name, your username, and your password, as shown in Figure 7.6. Choosing Local Network will display a text box where you can enter the path-name to the server, and a folder icon that will allow you to browse the LAN and locate the Web server.

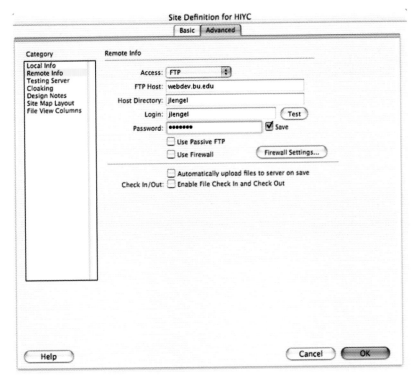

Figure 7.6 Defining the Remote Site

If you are using the FTP method, enter the required information, and then click the Test button. This will check to see if a connection can be made. If you entered the information correctly, your Internet connection is working, and the Web server is up and running, Dreamweaver will tell you that the connection was successful. Click OK, and from here on Dreamweaver will connect you automatically to the remote site when you update the pages.

If you are using the LAN method, use the folder icon to browse through the network to find the Web server. On large complex networks, you may need the Webmaster's help to show you where to find the Web server directory. You will need your username and password at some point in this process, either when you log in to the network, or when you make this connection. Once you have found the Web server, click the OK button at the bottom right of the Remote Site Definition dialog box, and Dreamweaver will be set to connect you to the server automatically as needed.

☆ **WARNING** **Network Connection**

Your computer must be connected to the Internet, with a valid IP address in order for the FTP method to work. For the LAN connection, your computer needs to be connected to the LAN and logged in.

Posting to the Server

Now that you have defined your remote site, you need to copy the Web site files to it from your local folder. In Dreamweaver, open your Site window by choosing Site→Site Files from the menubar. You will see your list of local files on the right and an empty column on the left, which is where the remote files will be displayed. To copy the files from the right column to the left, follow these steps:

1. Choose Connect from the Site menu.
2. Wait for the Web server directory to show in the left column.
3. Select your Web site folder in the right column.
4. Choose Put from the Site menu.
5. Watch your local site folder, and all of its contents, copy to the remote site.

☆ **SHORTCUT** **Use the Buttons**

Many of the menu commands in the Site window also can be accomplished by using the buttons at the top left of the window. Roll the mouse pointer over each button, and pause until its title is displayed, so that you know what each one does.

Testing the Remote Site

Once your site has been copied to the Web server, you should test its operation online. To do this, you'll need to know the URL of your site. URL stands for Universal Resource Locator, a string of characters that specifies the location of an item on the Internet. The URL of a Web site is the information you enter into the address bar of your Web browser. The URL for the *New York Times* Web site, for instance, is `http://www.nytimes.com`. Your Webmaster can tell you the URL of your site.

In most cases, the URL of your site will be `http://` plus the host name of your Web server (such as `www.bu.edu`), plus the pathname to your directory (perhaps `/students/`), plus the name of your site's folder (for example, `hiyc`). The URL for this example would be `http://www.bu.edu/students/hiyc`. To be sure, check with your Webmaster, since the FTP hostname and the URL may not be identical.

Once you know your site's URL, follow these steps to test it online:

1. Open your Web browser.

2. Enter the URL of your newly posted site into the address bar.

3. Press the return key on the keyboard.

4. Watch your home page appear in the browser.

If this try is unsuccessful, ask yourself these questions:

☆ Did I enter the URL exactly as I received it from the Webmaster?

☆ Is my home page saved as *index.html*? If not, you need to append the filename of the home page to the URL, such as `http://www.bu.edu/students/hiyc/myhome.html`.

☆ Did I enter the entire pathname correctly?

☆ Are all of my files and folders named correctly?

☆ Is my computer connected to the Internet? Try a well-known site to check.

As you review your site online, make note of any necessary changes. These notes will form the basis for revising and updating your site, as described in the next section of this chapter.

☆**TIP**　**Remote to Local**

Suppose you want to use Dreamweaver to edit and manage a site that's already posted on a Web server, but you have no local copy of it. This is possible, and not very difficult to do. Define a new site, and begin by setting the Remote Info. Enter the hostname, username, and password of the Web server into the Remote Info panel of the Site Definition dialog box. Click OK, and you will see the remote files—the ones on the Web server—in the left column. To copy them to the local list in the right column, first select the site folder from the remote side, and then choose Site→Get from the menubar. The files will be copied to the local side, and to your computer's disk.

◎◎ Remote Site Management

Once your remote site on the Web server is defined, posted, and operating, you can use Dreamweaver to manage the site. Few sites remain static—developed once and then left alone. Most sites change periodically, undergoing frequent editing and regular updating. With your site saved in two places—on your own computer (local), and on the Web server (remote)—this updating must be managed carefully.

With Dreamweaver, you may find it easiest to conduct this updating from the Site window, so that both sites can be updated in a coordinated fashion.

Updating the Site

When it is time to edit or update a page on your site—to add an event to the calendar, replace a picture, or add a new page—open your site by choosing Site→Open Site from the menubar and selecting your site.

> ☆**WARNING** **Multiple Users**
>
> If other people are using your computer to build their Web sites with Dreamweaver, or if you are managing more than one site, make sure that each time you launch Dreamweaver you open your own site. Otherwise the site last edited may remain as the chosen site in Dreamweaver, and your management may become fouled.

In the Site window's right (local) column, double-click the page you want to edit. The page will open in a Dreamweaver document window. Make the necessary changes, and then choose Save from the File menu. This will save the changes to the local copy of the site. Make changes as necessary to any of the other pages in the site, and then post your changes to the server as described in the next section of this chapter.

Site-Wide Changes

Sometimes you need to make a change on many or all pages of the site, such as when the organization's telephone number changes or a new menu item is added. Dreamweaver offers two methods to make these site-wide changes:

Templates. If you formatted your site with templates, you can make site-wide changes to any of the content in the repeating regions on a template page. To do this, open the template (.dwt) file from the *Templates* folder, make the changes, and save the file. This changes the local site. To see the changes reflected on the remote site, select the updated template file in the leftmost file list, and then choose Put from the Site menu.

Find and Replace. Dreamweaver can find and replace text anywhere on your site with a single click, whether you used templates, frames, tables, or no formatting at all. To find and replace text throughout the site, follow these steps:

1. Choose Edit→Find and Replace from the menubar.

2. From the Find In popup menu at the top of the Find and Replace dialog box, choose Entire current local site.

3. Enter the text you want to find in the upper box, and the new text you want to replace it with in the lower box, as shown in Figure 7.7.

4. Click the Replace All button.

5. Wait as Dreamweaver makes the changes throughout the local site.

6. Once the replacements are made, update the remote site by putting the modified files to the remote side.

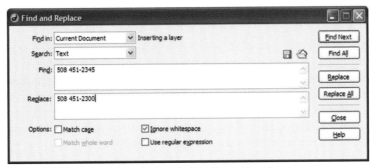

Figure 7.7 Finding and Replacing Text in the Entire Site

Checking Links

If you have made links between the pages of your site, you can let Dreamweaver check them all for you to see if they actually connect. After you've updated and modified the pages of your site, it's a good idea to check all of your links. To do this, open your Site window, and then choose Site→Check Links Sitewide from the menubar. Dreamweaver will display a results window, as shown in Figure 7.8, that will point out any broken links. Double-clicking the files with the bad links will open them in a Dreamweaver document window so that you can fix them.

Figure 7.8 Checking Links Sitewide

Posting Changes to the Server

When you modify or update files on the local site, you must remember to update these same files on the remote site. Dreamweaver does not do this automatically for you, but provides tools that make it easy. You can use any of the following three methods to post the files from the local site to the remote site:

☆ *Drag the files in the Site window.* Drag the updated files from the right (local) column to the left (remote) column. Dreamweaver will make a connection to the remote site and replace the old file on the remote site with the updated file.

☆ *Put the files on the server.* Select the files you have updated in the right (local) column in the Site window. Then choose Site→Put from the menubar.

Dreamweaver will connect to the Web server and copy the selected files to the remote site.

 Synchronize the sites. With your Site window open, choose Site→Synchronize from the menubar. In the Synchronize Files dialog box, choose Entire site, and Put newer files to remote from the popup menus. Dreamweaver will connect to the remote site, and check to see if if any of the files on the local site have been updated more recently than their counterparts on the remote site. If they need updating, Dreamweaver will do it for you. (Make sure the time and date on your own computer are correct.)

Whenever you post files to the Web server, no matter which method you use, take a moment to check the remote site online with the browser, as discussed earlier in this chapter.

You will find that the Dreamweaver's Site window and the items under the Site menu can make the task of managing a Web site easier and quicker. Like a fleet of ships, a well-managed site sails in a coordinated pattern, with clear communication between the elements, so that it can efficiently accomplish its mission.

☆ Summary

▷ Efficient Web site management begins with good planning: A clear statement of the audience and purpose of your site, and a detailed flow chart, are essential first steps.

▷ Once planned, a site must be organized by setting up folders, gathering the media elements for the site, and saving them in proper form to the folders.

▷ To take full advantage of Dreamweaver's site management capabilities, you must define your site. This allows you to work with it in the Site Files and Site Map views.

▷ Dreamweaver can help you to connect to a Web server where you can define a remote site and copy your files to it. This is called publishing your site.

▷ Dreamweaver provides a variety of tools for updating, modifying, and synchronizing the local and remote copies of your site.

☆ Online References

A tutorial on site management with Dreamweaver, from Cornell University
`http://www.cit.cornell.edu/atc/materials/FLEX/sitemgtdw/intro.shtml`

Web Site management using Dreamweaver, from Tech Prep
`http://www.bham.wednet.edu/technology/webdesign1/Unit_5_Dreamweaver_Introduction/Module_2/Lesson_3_%20Maintenance.html`

Managing a site, from the Macromedia Dreamweaver support center
`http://www.macromedia.com/support/dreamweaver/manage.html`

Site management with Dreamweaver, from the University of Texas
`http://www.ischool.utexas.edu/technology/tutorials/webdev/siteman/index.html`

Site management with Dreamweaver, from iBoost
`http://www.iboost.com/build/software/dw/tutorial/791.htm`

☆ Review Questions

1. Why is it important to state clearly the audience and purpose of a site, and to draw a flow chart before building it with Dreamweaver?

2. Describe the kinds of information that should be included for each Web page in a site flow chart.

3. What must be considered when setting up and naming the folders that will organize a Web site, and when saving the media elements for the site?

4. Trace the process of defining a site with Dreamweaver. Include both local and remote sites.

5. Explain Dreamweaver's Site window and how you can use it to manage a Web site.

6. Explain three different ways to post files from the local site to the remote site with Dreamweaver.

☆ Hands-On Exercises

1. Develop an audience profile and a statement of purpose for a sample Web site. Include the demographics of the target audience, their reasons for connecting, and the organization's goals in publishing the site.

2. Draw a detailed flow chart for a sample Web site. Include a rectangle for each page, along with a brief description of the content and filename of each page. Use lines to show the links between pages.

3. Create appropriate folders for a sample Web site, and gather the media elements for the pages into the proper folder(s). Pay special attention to filenames that will work well on the Web.

4. Use Dreamweaver to define a local site on your computer's disk drive.

5. Obtain from a Webmaster the host name, username, and password for a Web server that you can use to publish your site. Then use Dreamweaver to define a remote site on that server.

6. Develop and test a sample Web site on the local disk, and then use Dreamweaver to publish the site to the remote server. Test the site online with a browser to ensure its proper operation.

7. Use Dreamweaver's Site window to modify and update the pages of your local site. Then update the remote site in three different ways: by dragging, by putting, and by synchronizing the files.

BELLS AND WHISTLES

Add Whistles and Bells

To help sailors navigate, the Coast Guard places buoys in the water to mark the channels and warn of dangers. Most of the buoys are simple red and green floats, which have been used for centuries to guide the seafarer, and they serve their purpose quite well. But a few buoys are fitted with bells, whistles, or blinking lights to make them easier to find and to distinguish them from the standard buoys. The whistles and bells are not necessary to basic navigation, but they sure make the sailor's life easier.

In the same way, most Web sites work well without fancy rollover buttons, photo albums, or interactive navigation bars. But under some circumstances, for some members of the audience, these extra devices can help make the Web site easier to use and more effective. This chapter teaches you about a few of the tools that Dreamweaver provides to help you create the additional features.

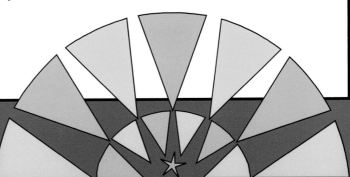

◎◎ Chapter Objectives

☆ To be able to use Dreamweaver to create interactive rollover buttons with both JavaScript and Flash

☆ To learn how to build an interactive navigation bar with Dreamweaver

☆ To create a Web photo album of images using Dreamweaver and Fireworks

☆ To learn how to embed anchors and create an interactive table of contents for long text documents on a Web page

☆ To be able to embed links in a document that open an email window addressed to a specific person

☆ To understand how to import tabular data from an Excel document into a table in Dreamweaver

☆ To be able to add a background color or background image to a Web page

◎◎ Extra Features

Like the bells, whistles, and lights on navigational buoys, extra features on a Web site can make it easier for members of your audience to see what they need on the page and find their way through your site. Few sites will take advantage of all of these features, but most commercial Web sites use at least two or three of them. As you prepare to work through this chapter, browse the Web and look for an example of each of these devices.

You may find a few sites where the extra features are overdone, with buttons blinking, navigation bars flashing, and bandwidth-robbing slides showing at every turn. Be careful as you use these features in your own site, and make sure there's a good reason for employing each one. For instance, if the audience can navigate just as well with static menu items, then there's no need to build rollover buttons. On the other hand, to better understand the capabilities of Dreamweaver, you should take the time to learn how to use these extra features. It's a good idea to try building each of them into your own sample site so that you can see how they work.

A few of the extra features, such as the rollover buttons, photo album, and the import of tabular data require that you have installed on your computer other software programs, such as Adobe Photoshop, Macromedia Fireworks, and Microsoft Excel. The rest can be accomplished with Dreamweaver alone.

◎◎ Adding Rollover Buttons

A rollover button is a navigational device that changes as the user rolls the mouse pointer over it. It's most commonly seen in menu choices: When you roll the mouse over a menu selection on the Web page, it seems to light up or change color to indicate that it's a clickable item. And when you click it, it opens a new Web page. Dreamweaver offers two ways of building these kinds of buttons—with Flash or with JavaScript. You do not need to know how to program with either of these methods; Dreamweaver does the programming for you. You don't need to own the Flash application or a JavaScript editor, either; these capabilities are built into Dreamweaver. Flash buttons are faster and easier to create, but require the Flash player, while JavaScript buttons are more versatile.

Adding Flash Buttons

A Flash button contains text on a graphic background. When rolled over, the button changes color, and when clicked, it links to another Web page. To build a Flash button, you need to know the text of the button and the URL of the page you wish to link to. A Flash button can be placed anywhere on the page, embedded in the text, appearing in the cell of a table, or inserted as the contents of a layer. To build a Flash button, you need an already existing Web page that has been saved in proper form. Follow these steps to add a simple Flash button to a page:

1. Open the page in a Dreamweaver Document window.
2. Place the cursor where you want the button to appear.
3. Choose Insert→Interactive Images→Flash button from the menubar.
4. In the Insert Flash Button dialog box, as shown in Figure 8.1:
   a. Select the style of the button from the list.
   b. Enter the text of the button.
   c. Select the font of the text from the popup menu.
   d. Enter the size of the text into the box.
   e. Enter (or browse to) the page you want this button to link to.
   f. Enter the name of the target frame or window, if any.
   g. Select a background color for the button by clicking the Bg color button, if any.
   h. Enter a name for this button in the Save As box. Each button on your site must have a unique name.
   i. Click the OK button in the upper right of the dialog box.
5. Watch the Flash button appear on your Web page.
6. Test the operation of the Flash button by previewing the page in the browser.

The button created by Figure 8.1 would look like the button shown in Figure 8.2.

These buttons exhibit different behaviors when rolled over, depending on their style. For instance, when the user rolls over the button shown in Figure 8.2, the star spins. Other styles flash, blink, and change color when rolled over or when clicked. Some even make noise. Experiment with different styles to see what's possible. To change the style, color, or text of a Flash button that you have already created, double-click it in the Dreamweaver document window. (Not all of the styles allow changes.)

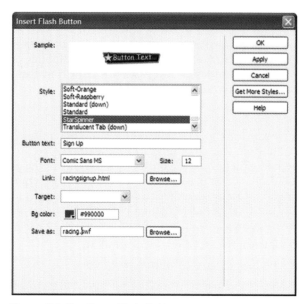

Figure 8.1 Creating a Flash Button

Figure 8.2 Sample Flash Button

Because these buttons are made with Flash's vector graphics, you can stretch and shrink them without spoiling their looks or pixilation. But be careful to make sure that when you create a series of Flash buttons to be used perhaps for a menu list, they all maintain exactly the same size.

These Flash buttons are saved into your Web site folder as Flash movies, with the .swf filename extension. Like other images or animations that are used in your site, the Flash button files must stay in the same folder with the same filename, both in your local site and in your remote site.

Adding Javascript Buttons

Dremweaver can also construct a different type of rollover button for you, made with Javascript. These are called *rollover images* in Dreamweaver. They are best used for buttons based on icons or images rather than text. They take longer to make and are more difficult to edit, but they are more flexible in their possibilities.

Prepare the Images

To create this kind of button, first you need to prepare two images, an *original* and a *rollover* image. These two images should be exactly the same size. When the user rolls over the original image, the rollover image appears in its place. When she rolls off, the original image reappears. These images should be prepared in an image-editing program such as Photoshop or Fireworks, and saved in your Web site folder in one of the standard Web image formats such as GIF, PNG, or JPEG, as described in Chapter Three.

Figure 8.3 shows two images prepared in Photoshop—they might also be prepared in Fireworks or another image-editor—for use in a JavaScript button for our sample Web site. This button will be used to link to the sign-up form for the sailboat race. The rollover image (sail_btn2.gif) is the same size as the original image (sail_btn1.gif), but differs in the angle of the boat, the color of the sails, and the presence of the text.

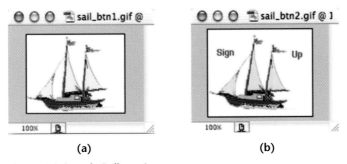

(a)   (b)

Figure 8.3 Sample Rollover Images

The best way to learn this process is to construct the buttons as you read, so create two images for your own sample. You can use an image-editing program, or download two appropriate images from the Web. Make sure they are the same size.

Insert the Images

Follow these steps to create a rollover button from the images you have prepared:

1. On the Dreamweaver Document window, place the cursor where you want the image to appear.

2. Choose Insert→Interactive Images→Rollover Image from the menubar.

3. In the Insert Rollover Image dialog box, enter the necessary information, as illustrated in Figure 8.4:

   a. The name of the rollover button, for your reference only

   b. The filename of the original image (browse to this)

   c. The filename of the rollover image (browse to this)

   d. The alternative text for the button (you don't need this, but it makes your page more accessible)

   e. The filename of the page to link to (browse to this)

4. Click OK, and you will see the original image on the page.

5. Test the operation of the rollover image by previewing the page in the browser.

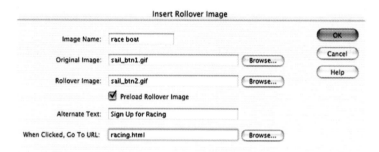

Figure 8.4 Insert Rollover Dialog Box

☆ **TIP**   **Alternative Text**

Every image in your Web site, including the rollover images, should include a text message that will be displayed for viewers who cannot or choose not to view images on their browser. These include people with vision impairments, users connecting on text-only devices such as PDAs and mobile phones, and those who have turned image display off on their browsers to conserve bandwidth. Enter the ALT text into the Properties window of the image.

To make the rollover image operate in the browser, Dreamweaver uses JavaScript. For the example shown in Figures 8.3 and 8.4, the code first defines the functions MM_swapImgRestore and MM_swapImage, in the HEAD portion of the HTML page:

```
function MM_swapImgRestore() { //v3.0
   var i,x,a=document.MM_sr;
   for(i=0;a&&i<a.length&&(x=a[i])&&x.oSrc;i++) x.src=x.oSrc;
}
```

```
function MM_swapImage() { //v3.0
  var i,j=0,x,a=MM_swapImage.arguments;
  document.MM_sr=new Array;
for(i=0;i<(a.length-2);i+=3)
  if ((x=MM_findObj(a[i]))!=null){document.MM_sr[j++]=x;
  if(!x.oSrc) x.oSrc=x.src; x.src=a[i+2];}
}
```

Then in the body of the HTML, the code inserts the original image in an HREF link, and calls on the two swapping functions when the mouse is rolled over and out:

```
<a href="racing.html"
onMouseOut="MM_swapImgRestore()"
onMouseOver="MM_swapImage('sail btn','','sail_btn2.gif',1)">
<img src="sail_btn1.gif" alt="Sign Up for the Race"
name="sail btn" width="139" height="108" border="0"></a>
```

Dreamweaver does this scripting automatically. You do not need to understand this code to create rollover images with Dreamweaver. To learn more about JavaScript and how it works to produce this kind of interactive image, consult *The Web Wizard's Guide to JavaScript.*

◎◉ Making an Interactive Navigation Bar

An interactive navigation bar is similar to a rollover image—it's actually a collection of several rollover images that appear together. In the sample Web site we have been using in this book, we can make the menu items on the left into a vertical navigation bar. Once constructed, this navigation bar is easily inserted into all the pages of a site. When you roll over an item on the nav bar, it changes appearance, and when you click, it links to another page.

To make such a bar, you should first prepare four images for each menu item:

☆ An *up* image that appears when the page opens.

☆ An *over* image that appears when the user rolls the mouse pointer over the menu item.

☆ A *down* image that appears when the user holds the mouse button down on the menu item.

☆ An *over while down* image that appears when the user rolls over the image with the mouse down.

These images can be prepared in Photoshop or Fireworks as described above in the section *Adding JavaScript Buttons,* and saved in your Web site folder. When saving them, choose filenames that explain what these images are, as shown in Figure 8.5. So for our sample site, with five menu items, we'd prepare 20 different images for our navigation bar. To try this out for yourself, prepare the images you need for your nav bar.

☆ **SHORTCUT   You Really Only Need Two Images**

While the Dreamweaver navigation bar toolkit allows four different images as described above, you don't have to prepare all four if you don't need them. An effective nav bar can be made with just two images for each menu item, an *up* image and an *over* image.

With all the images prepared, open a Web page in Dreamweaver. Place the cursor where you want the nav bar to appear. Then choose Insert→Interactive Images→Navigation Bar from the menubar. You will see the Navigation Bar dialog box as in Figure 8.5.

Figure 8.5 Creating a Navigation Bar

Into the spaces in the dialog box enter the information for your navigation bar:

1. The Nav Bar Elements are the various menu items you need. The names you enter here are for your reference only—the audience will not see them. Enter the names in the Element Name box just below the Nav Bar Elements box.

2. For each element that you name, you must choose an Up Image. This is best done by browsing to the image file that you prepared earlier.

3. If you want any interactivity at all, you'll also need an Over Image for the item. Browse to this file as well.

4. You can also enter a Down Image and an Over While Down Image, but you don't have to.

5. You should enter an Alternate Text for the menu item, usually the name of the page it links to.

6. You must enter a link in the box next to Go to URL. This is the page that will be loaded when the user clicks the item. You can also enter a target frame or window for this link.

7. Repeat steps 2–6 for each of the elements of your nav bar.

8. Click OK when the nav bar is complete.

9. Watch the nav bar appear on the page.

10. Test the nav bar by previewing the page in the browser.

To edit the nav bar after it's been tested, select it on the page, and then choose Modify→Navigation Bar from the menubar.

◎◎ Making a Web Photo Album

A photo album on the Web can be a powerful way to communicate ideas to your audience. From what you learned in Chapter Three of this book, you could construct a Web photo album by creating a page for each photo, inserting an image onto each page, and creating forward and back buttons with links to the next photo in the series. You could also format a menu page with a thumbnail of each image. This would involve a considerable amount of work.

Dreamweaver offers an automated command to make such a photo album. This feature relies on Macromedia Fireworks for its operation, so make sure you have installed Fireworks if you plan to try this. As an example, we will build a photo album from a series of digital photos of the HIYC annual cruise, sent in by the various cruisers. All of the images have been placed in a folder called *BYC Cruise 03* on the computer's hard disk. Here are the steps we will use to make a Web photo album from these images:

1. Open Dreamweaver.

2. Choose Commands→Create Web Photo Album from the menubar.

3. Enter a name for your photo album, which will become the title of the Web page.

4. Enter a subhead for the show if needed.

5. Browse to the folder that will serve as the source of the images.

6. Browse to your Web site folder, and create a new folder to receive the photo album.

7. Leave the rest of the settings as they are.

8. Click OK to create the photo album.

9. Watch as Dreamweaver opens Fireworks, modifies your images as necessary, and creates the pages of the Web photo album.

The photo album files—several HTML pages and several image files—will be in the folder you created for it. Test it in the browser to see how it works.

For viewers of your Web site to see the photo album, you must:

☆ Copy the photo album folder to your remote site on the Web server.

☆ Make a link from an existing page on your site to the menu page of the photo album.

◎◎ Using Anchors

Sometimes you need to include a long text document in a Web site, such as the bylaws of the Hog Island Yacht Club. It's easy to use Dreamweaver to paste the entire text of the document into a long scrolling page, but this long page may be difficult to use. What if the reader wants to quickly find the section on the election of officers? You can help your audience find what they need on these types of pages by using *anchors*.

An anchor is a hidden marker in the text that the browser can link to. In most cases, you'd place an anchor at the beginning of each section of the document. Then, at the top of the page, you'd add a little outline of the sections. Each item in this outline would be a hypertext link to the anchor it represents. When the user clicks the item in the outline, the page scrolls down to the appropriate section. The outline serves as an interactive index to the entire document.

Here's how to set up anchors and an index:

1. Create a Web page with a long text document.

2. If the document doesn't have them already, add subheads for each section, and use bold style and a larger size to contrast the subheads with the rest of the text.

3. Place the cursor in front of the subhead of a section of the document.

4. Choose Insert→Named Anchor from the menubar.

5. Enter a name for the anchor, and click OK. Keep names to a single word, as shown in Figure 8.6.

6. Watch as Dreamweaver inserts an anchor symbol on the page. (Only you will see this symbol—it will be invisible to your audience. If you can't see the symbol, choose View→Visual Aids→Invisible Elements and make sure they are checked.)

7. Repeat steps 3–5 for the remaining sections of the document. Keep a record of the anchor names that you assign.

8. At the top of the page, create an outline of the sections of the document, as shown in Figure 8.7.

9. Link each item in the outline to its corresponding anchor, as follows:

- Select the item in the outline.
- In the Properties window, enter "#" plus the name of the anchor, as shown in Figure 8.7.
- Repeat this process for each item in the outline.

10. Test the operation of the index and anchors by previewing the page in the browser.

Figure 8.6 Naming Anchors

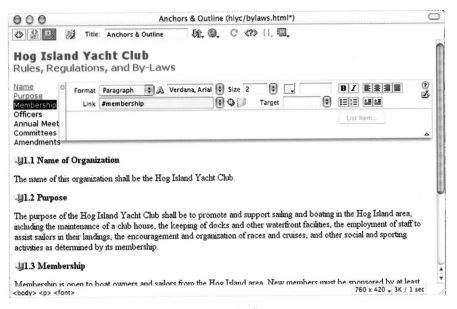

Figure 8.7 Creating and Linking a Document Outline

◎◎ Creating Email Links

Earlier in this book, you learned how to use Dreamweaver to make hypertext links to pages in your own site, or to other sites on the Web. You can also make a link that lets the user send an email to you or someone else in your organization. For instance, on the membership page in the Hog Island Yacht Club site, we might want to include in the text a phrase such as "For answers to your questions about the membership process, send an email to Joseph Conrad, HIYC Membership Committee Chairman." When the user clicks on the blue underlined text, we want to open his email application with a message pre-addressed to Mr. Conrad. Here's how this can be done with Dreamweaver:

1. Create a Web page with some text or an image that you want to open an email link.

2. Select the text or image to link from.

3. Choose Insert→Email link from the menubar.

4. Enter the email address of the recipient into the lower box, as shown in Figure 8.8.

5. Click OK, and Dreamweaver will set up the link.

6. To test the email link, preview the page in the browser:

   a. Choose File→Preview in Browser from the menubar.

   b. Watch as the page opens.

   c. Click the email link you just made.

   d. You should see your email application (such as Outlook, Eudora, or Mail) open, and a new message window open, addressed to the recipient you entered.

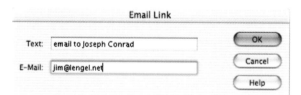

Figure 8.8 Creating an Email Link

☆**WARNING** **Browser Email Preferences**

Emailing from a Web page will not work unless you have configured your browser to work with your email application. In many cases, especially with recently purchased computers, this is taken care of by the manufacturer. If not, open your browser's preference panel, select the email preferences, and enter your email address as well as your email server name.

◎◎ Importing and Displaying Tabular Data

Each Wednesday after the Hog Island Yacht Club weekly race, the results are calculated using a spreadsheet, and the winners in each class are listed, along with handicaps and finish times. With about 40 boats in the race, in five different classes, this is quite a bit of information presented in many rows and columns. And the racers want this on the HIYC Web site by Thursday!

Dreamweaver makes this easy. Tabular data, such as what you see in an Excel spreadsheet, can be directly imported into a table in a Dreamweaver document. Calendars, schedules, results of sporting events, product specifications, and other information commonly prepared in a spreadsheet can easily be included and updated on your Web site. Follow these steps:

1. Use Excel or another spreadsheet program to prepare the information. Do not bother with formatting the text at this time.

2. Export the spreadsheet data as a tab-delimited text file, as shown in Figure 8.9:

    a. Choose File➔Save As from the menubar.

    b. In the dialog box, set the format to Text (Tab delimited).

    c. Save the file to a convenient location.

3. Open with Dreamweaver the Web page on which you wish to display the tabular data.

4. Place the cursor where you want the data to appear.

5. Choose Insert➔Table Objects➔Import Tabular Data from the menubar.

6. In the Import Tabular Data dialog box, browse to the data file you just saved from Excel, and click the Open button.

7. Click OK in the Import Tabular Data dialog box, as shown in Figure 8.10.

8. Watch as the information appears in a table in the Web page.

9. Edit and format the text in the table as necessary.

10. Preview the page in the browser.

Figure 8.9 Saving Spreadsheet Data

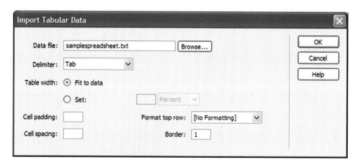

Figure 8.10 Importing Tabular Data

Figure 8.11 shows a sample Excel spreadsheet, and Figure 8.12 shows these data as they appear in a Dreamweaver document.

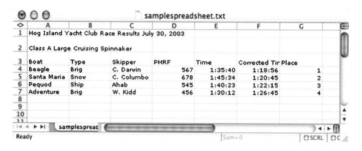

Figure 8.11 Sample Spreadsheet

Figure 8.12 Sample Table of Data

◎◎ Background Colors and Images

So far in this book all of the pages you have built display plain white backgrounds. This is good for easy reading, but there are times when you'd like to see a solid color or a picture appear in the background of a page. Dreamweaver makes it easy to use these unusual backgrounds, but be careful—it's much more difficult for your audience to read text on a colored background, or on top of an image. This is one bell or whistle that can make a Web page less useful if you are not careful.

Background Color

To set a background color on a page, choose Modify→Page Properties from the menubar. This opens a Page Properties dialog box, in which you can set a background color and other attributes of the page, as shown in Figure 8.13. Use the button labeled Background to choose a color for the page. Light colors work best under pages that will display text.

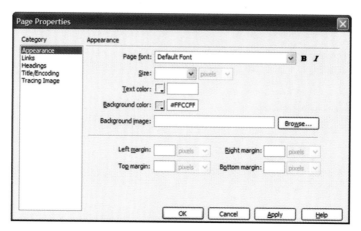

Figure 8.13 Setting Page Background Color

☆ **TIP   Page Title**

While you are working in the Page Properties dialog box, it's a good idea to enter a title for the page. The title is different from the filename; the title appears in the title bar at the top of the browser window. A page does not need a title in order to work on the Web, but it's a good way to let the user know what he's looking at. Keep the title short and simple.

Background Image

Two kinds of background images are commonly found on Web sites:

☆ Large, screen-filling pictures, often very washed out photographs that appear once on the page.

☆ Small images, often logos, that appear over and over across and down the page. These are called *tiled background images*.

No matter which type of image you need, the first step is to prepare the image, using a program such as Photoshop. In most cases, the image should be lightened considerably, and its contrast reduced, so that it appears washed out in the background. This can be done by choosing Image→Adjustments→Brightness/Contrast from the Photoshop menubar, and then using the sliders to adjust brightness and contrast until the desired result is achieved, as shown in Figure 8.14.

Small tiled images can appear at any size you choose, but for the screen-filling image, size is critical. These large images must be big enough to fill the browser window of your typical user. For the sample illustrated in this chapter, we made the image 1000 pixels wide and 750 pixels high, by choosing Image→Image Size from Photoshop's menubar. The background image should be saved in your Web site folder.

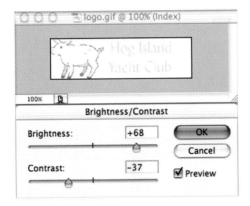

Figure 8.14 Adjusting Background Image in Photoshop

The second step is to set this image as the background of your Web page. Follow these steps:

1. Open a Web page in Dreamweaver.
2. Choose Modify→Page Properties from the menubar.
3. In the Page Properties dialog box, browse to the background image you just saved, as shown in Figure 8.15.
4. Watch the background image appear behind the other content of your Web page.

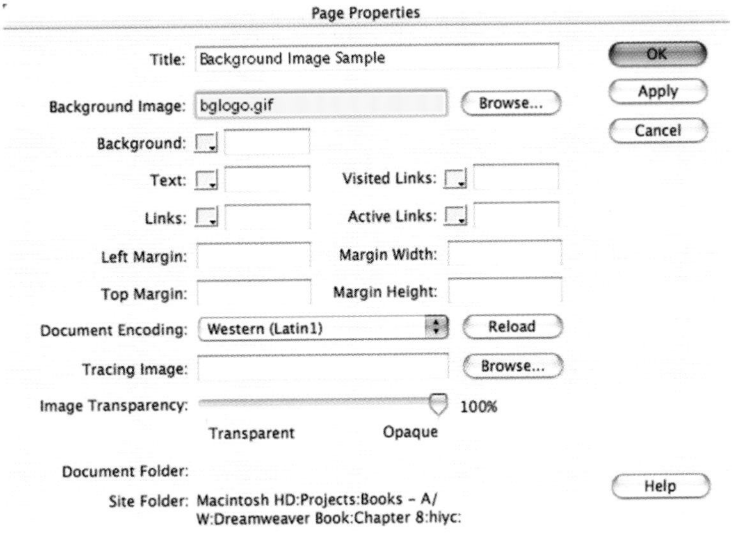

Figure 8.15 Setting Background Image

Figure 8.16 shows the result of setting a small logo as a tiled background image on the race results page we used recently as a sample. Notice how the information in the table has become a bit more difficult to read.

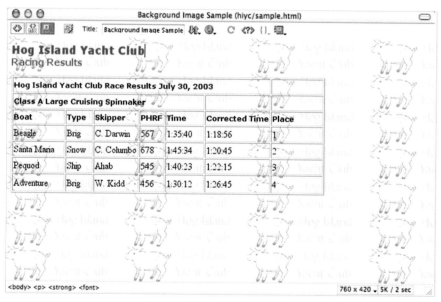

Figure 8.16 Tiled Background Image

This page might work better with a large, screen-filling image, as shown in Figure 8.17.

◎◎ Bells and Whistles

Imagine a Web page that used every one of the devices described in this chapter. It would be quite a hodge-podge of elements, and because of the distractive properties of some of the devices, the page might fail to communicate its essential message to the audience. So be careful when adding bells and whistles to your site. The important thing to know is that Dreamweaver is fully capable of helping you to add the touches that can help your site sail to new places.

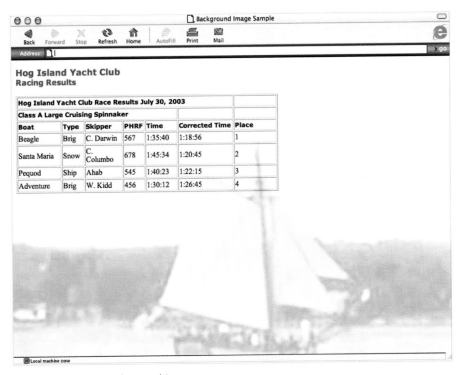

Figure 8.17 Large Background Image

☆ Summary

- ▷ Extra features can help a Web site accomplish its purpose, but you must take care not to overload your pages with distracting visual devices.

- ▷ Rollover buttons can be created in Dreamweaver in two ways: as Flash buttons or as rollover JavaScript images.

- ▷ Dreamweaver can help you create a navigation bar that provides a single consistent menu scheme for a site, with rollover interaction.

- ▷ Dreamweaver can create a Web photo album from a collection of images automatically, using Fireworks.

- ▷ Long text pages can be made more useful with an index at the top and anchors throughout the text.

- ▷ An email link can allow users of a site to make a direct email connection from a link on the page.

- ▷ Dreamweaver can import tabular data from an Excel spreadsheet directly into an HTML table on a Web page.

- ▷ Dreamweaver makes it easy to place solid colors or images into the background of a Web page.

☆ Online References

Tutorial on Dreamweaver Flash buttons, from Vecpix
`http://www.vecpix.com/tutorials/dreamweaver/dw002.php`

Creating rollover buttons with Dreamweaver and Fireworks, from SmartWebby
`http://www.smartwebby.com/web_site_design/rollover_images.asp`

Make a dynamic navigation bar with Dreamweaver MX, from TechTV
`http://www.techtv.com/screensavers/answertips/story/0,24330,3391885,00.html`

Navigation bar overview for Dreamweaver, from Macromedia
`http://www.macromedia.com/support/dreamweaver/programs/navbar_overview/`

Named anchors from Dreamweaver FAQ
`http://www.dwfaq.com/Tutorials/Basics/named_anchors.asp`

Creating email links with Dreamweaver, from the Lewis Center
`http://lewiscenter.org/force/1044/subprojects/hyper.php`

Importing tabular data into Dreamweaver, from Macromedia
`http://sdc.shockwave.com/support/dreamweaver/assets/`
`importing_spread/importing_spread02.html`

☆ Review Questions

1. Describe the differences between the two methods of creating rollover buttons in Dreamweaver: the Flash button method and the JavaScript rollover images method.

2. How many different images would you need to prepare for a navigation bar with five menu items? Why? What must be considered when creating these images?

3. Describe the steps in the process of creating a Web photo album with Dreamweaver.

4. How do anchors and an index assist the user in navigating long text documents on the Web?

5. How can information from a spreadsheet most easily be incorporated in a Web page?

6. Describe the process of placing background colors and background images on a Web page.

7. What are some possible drawbacks of using "bells and whistles" on a Web page?

☆ Hands-On Exercises

1. Browse the Web to find pages that use each of the devices mentioned in this chapter. In what ways do these bells and whistles enhance the viewer's experience? In what ways do they distract her from the main message of the site?

2. Develop a sample Web page with five Flash buttons and five rollover images. Describe the difference in both user experience and developer work process for the two types of buttons.

3. Prepare an interactive navigation bar for your sample Web site, with up, over, and down images for each of at least five menu items.

4. From a set of digital photos, use Dreamweaver to create a Web photo album with at least six pictures.

5. Insert named anchors in a Web page that contains a long text document of at least three pages. Develop subheads as necessary, as well as an interactive index at the top of the page that links to the anchors.

6. Develop an email link in a sample Web page. Test it with the browser to ensure its operation.

7. Create a sample Web page with a well-designed background image.

APPENDIX: ANSWERS TO ODD-NUMBERED REVIEW QUESTIONS

Chapter One

1. Dreamweaver can help you lay out a Web page, insert various media elements into a page, edit text, make links, post files to a Web server, and manage a Web site. Dreamweaver cannot create or edit images, sounds, videos, or animation, nor can it serve Web pages to your audience.

3. For images: Adobe Photoshop, Photoshop Elements, PaintShop Pro, and Macromedia Fireworks. For sound: Macromedia SoundEdit, CoolEdit Pro, SoundForge, Peak, and Deck. For video: Final Cut Pro, iMovie, Adobe Premiere, QuickTime Player Pro, and Windows MovieMaker. For animation: Macromedia Flash, GIF Animator, GIFBuilder, and Fireworks.

5. First, prepare the image in a format proper for the Web. Second, save it to your Web site folder with an acceptable filename. Third, place the cursor where you want the image to appear. Fourth, choose Insert→Image from the menubar.

7. First, select the text or image you want to link from. Second, choose Modify→Make Link from the menubar. Third, choose the page or enter the URL of the page you want to link to. Fourth, test the link in the browser.

Chapter Two

1. If the text for the Web page exists already in a Microsoft Word document, or if you want others to format the text in advance, then it's best to do the preparation in Word. If you are entering text from scratch, or copying and pasting it from another source, then it's best to enter it directly into Dreamweaver.

3. Keep the sentences and paragraphs and pages short. Make sure the writing is self-contained, with each section able to stand by itself. Write in a straightforward style, with active verbs and clear phrasing. Use subheads liberally to help the reader find the information she needs as she scrolls through the text. Use hypertext links to send readers to other sites for more detail.

5. Choose a font family from the list provided by Dreamweaver, rather than a specific unusual font that your audience may not possess. Use no more than two font families on a page. Use bold and italic sparingly, and only when absolutely necessary. Contrast font and style between subheads and body text. Set the width of the text to achieve 10 to 12 words per line.

7. You can insert a table with Dreamweaver, and then enter or paste the data directly into the cells of the table. You can also import tabular data from a tab-delimited text file saved from an Excel spreadsheet. Use the Insert→Table Objects→Import Tabular Data command from the menubar. For ease of reading, numeric data should be aligned to the right.

◎◎ Chapter Three

1. First, plan how and where your images will appear on the page. Second, prepare your images with an image editor, and save them in the proper size, resolution, and file format for the Web, with an acceptable filename. Third, insert the images into your Web page. Fourth, align your image with the other items on the page, as necessary. Fifth, create any necessary links or image maps from your image. Finally, test your work in a browser.

3. Images should be saved in the proper file format (JPEG, GIF, or PNG) into the correct Web site folder, with an appropriate amount of data compression and an acceptable filename and extension.

5. You can use the text alignment tools to place the image to the left, in the center, or to the right. You can also set the align attribute of the image to make it appear to the left or the right of the text on the page. Or, for more control over appearance, you can create a table on the page and insert the image into one of its cells, and then adjust the table to achieve the desired alignment.

7. Linking from an image causes a single link to be made when the user clicks anywhere on the image. An image map allows multiple different links from a single image, by creating several hotspots on the image.

◎◎ Chapter Four

1. For images: Adobe Photoshop, Photoshop Elements. PaintShop Pro, and Macromedia Fireworks. For sound: Macromedia SoundEdit, CoolEdit Pro, SoundForge, Peak, and Deck. For video: Final Cut Pro, iMovie, Adobe Premiere, QuickTime Player Pro, and Windows MovieMaker. For animation: Macromedia Flash, GIF Animator, GIFBuilder, and Fireworks.

3. First, plan the animation, in terms of its purpose, size, and duration. Second, prepare the animation with an appropriate animation editor. Third, save it in proper format with an acceptable filename to your Web site folder. Fourth, insert it into the Web page. Fifth, test its operation in the browser.

5. Embedded media displays itself within the Web page, among the other elements of the page, in the same browser window. Linked media displays itself in a new browser or player window, separate from (and often hiding) the other elements on the page.

7. The appearance of these elements can be adjusted by altering their height and width attributes, and by aligning them with the other elements on the page. User control can be accomplished by specifying a controller during the inserting process, and setting the autoplay parameter to false.

◎◎ Chapter Five

1. Forms can be used to register for a product or event, such as online software registration. Forms can also be used to collect feedback from the site's audience, such as a viewer comment or question form. They can be used to enter data, such as a product purchase site, or can enable a viewer to provide information for a survey or poll. Finally, forms can be used to enter keywords for a search engine such as Google.

3. A text field collects short sequences of words and numbers. A text area collects sentences and paragraphs. A radio button collects a mutually exclusive forced choice among items. A check box collects numerous choices from a list. And a popup menu collects one item from a list of choices.

5. A form needs a layout table if it contains more than a few form objects. This makes the form easier to read and complete.

7. To test the operation of a form, you must view the form page in a browser. Dreamweaver cannot test the operation of a form.

◎◎ Chapter Six

1. You can format a page with tables, templates, frames, or layers.

3. First, sketch a plan of your page, showing where the various elements will appear. Then, determine which layout method is appropriate for this page design and for your audience. Next, determine the sizes, in pixels, of the various parts of the layout. Now you are ready to set up your page.

5. First, plan the layout. Second, determine the number of rows and columns in the table, and the sizes of each. Third, insert the table into the page. Fourth, adjust the sizes of the cells in the table to fit your plan. Fifth, merge or split cells as necessary. Sixth, insert or enter the various elements into the cells of the table.

7. The frameset page simply sets forth the position, size, and component pages of the various frames—it contains no content visible to the viewer. The component pages contain the visible content, and are displayed in one of the frames of the frameset.

◎◎ Chapter Seven

1. Unless you clearly define the audience for your Web site, you will not have enough information to make good decisions about content, design, use of media, and other aspects of the site. If you have not defined its purpose, you will have difficulty organizing the content and planning the structure.

3. First you need to consider how big your site will be. A site of only a few pages will not need subfolders. But any site with many pages and many media files should have a folder (or folders) for the images, sound, animation, and video files that will be used on the pages. Folders should be named with simple filenames that are acceptable to the Web.

5. The Site window shows a list of files for the local site (on your computer), and another for the remote site (on the server). You can use the Site window to access your files to work on them, to move files from the local to the remote site, and to check their synchronization.

◎◎ Chapter Eight

1. It's quite a bit simpler to create a Flash button. Just select from a list of button styles, add text and a URL, and the button is made. For JavaScript rollover buttons, first create images of the two states of the button in an image editor, and then save them. Then in Dreamweaver, use the rollover images dialog box to select the two files and choose a URL. Flash buttons need the Flash Player, while rollover buttons will work without a plug-in.

3. Before you start, make sure that Fireworks is installed on your computer. The Web Photo Album requires Fireworks. First, arrange your digital photo files into a folder on your disk. Then, in Dreamweaver, choose Commands→Create Web Photo Album from the menubar. Next, provide a name for your album, and select a folder to send it to (inside your Web folder). When you click OK, you will see the album being created.

5. The best way to incorporate data from a spreadsheet onto a Web page is to export the file from Excel as a tab-delimited text file. Then use Dreamweaver's Insert→Table Objects→Import Tabular Data item from the menubar. This will allow you to import the text file you saved from Excel and see it appear as a table in Dreamweaver.

7. Bells and whistles may distract your audience from the content and message of your Web site. They may cause longer download times, require plug-ins and players that your users do not have, and make navigation more complex. Building the bells and whistles may also take more of your time than necessary to publish an effective Web site.

INDEX

◉◎ Keyboard Shortcuts for Dreamweaver MX

Documents, Windows, and Files

Action	Windows	Macintosh
Open new document window	Ctrl + N	⌘ + N
Open a file	Ctrl + O	⌘ + O
Save a File	Ctrl + S	⌘ + V
Save File as	Ctrl + Shift + S	⌘ + Shift + S
Open Properties Window	Ctrl + F3	⌘ + F3
Open in frame	Ctrl + Shift + O	⌘ + Shift + O
Close Window	Ctrl + W	⌘ + W
Quit Dreamweaver	Ctrl + Q	⌘ + Q

General Commands

Action	Windows	Macintosh
Cut	Ctrl + X	⌘ + X
Copy	Ctrl + C	⌘ + C
Paste	Ctrl + V	⌘ + V
Clear	Del	Del
Undo	Ctrl + Z	⌘ + Z
Redo	Ctrl + Y	⌘ + Y

Editing Text

Action	Windows	Macintosh
Create a new paragraph	Enter	Return
Insert a line break 	Shift + Enter	Shift + Return
Select a word	Double-click	Double-click
Set Bold Style	Ctrl + B	⌘ + B
Set Italic Style	Ctrl + I	⌘ + I
Select All	Ctrl + A	⌘ + A
Move to start of line	Home	Home
Move to end of line	End	End
Select to start of line	Shift + Home	Shift + Home
Select to end of line	Shift + End	Shift + End
Go to next/previous word	Ctrl + →/←	⌘ + →/←
Go to next/previous paragraph	Ctrl + ↑/↓	⌘ + ↑/↓
Delete word left	Ctrl + Backspace	⌘ + Backspace
Delete word right	Ctrl + Del	⌘ + Del
Find and Replace	Ctrl + F	⌘ + F
Find next/find again	F3	⌘ + G
Replace	Ctrl + H	⌘ + H
Check spelling	Shift + F7	Shift + F7

Formatting Text

Action	Windows	Macintosh
Indent	Ctrl + Alt +]	⌘ + Option +]
Outdent	Ctrl + Alt + [	⌘ + Option + [
Format > None	Ctrl + 0 (zero)	⌘ + 0 (zero)
Paragraph Format	Ctrl + Shift + P	⌘ + Shift + P
Apply Headings 1 through 6 to a paragraph	Ctrl + 1 through 6	⌘ + 1 through 6
Align > Left/Center/ Right/Justify	Ctrl + Alt + Shift + L/C/R/J	⌘ + Alt + Shift + L/C/R/J

Making Links

Action	Windows	Macintosh
Create hyperlink (select text or object)	Ctrl + L	⌘ + L
Remove hyperlink	Ctrl + Shift + L	⌘ + Shift + L

Working with Tables

Action	Windows	Macintosh
Select table (with cursor inside the table)	Ctrl + A	⌘ + A
Move to the next cell	Tab	Tab
Move to the previous cell	Shift + Tab	Shift + Tab
Insert a row (before current row)	Ctrl + M	⌘ + M
Add a row at end of table	Tab in the last cell	Tab in the last cell
Delete the current row	Ctrl + Shift + M	⌘ + Shift + M
Insert a column	Ctrl + Shift + A	⌘ + Shift + A
Delete a column	Ctrl + Shift + − (hyphen)	⌘ + Shift + − (hyphen)
Merge selected table cells	Ctrl + Alt + M	⌘ + Option + M
Split table cell	Ctrl + Alt + S	⌘ + Option + S

CREDITS

Web-Safe Colors

Most computers can display millions of colors, but they do not display all colors consistently. For example, one computer may display a Web page with a dark red background, whereas another displays the same Web page with a brown background. To ensure that your Web pages look the same to everyone, select your colors from the following palette of 216 Web-safe colors. These colors will always look the same (or at least very close to the same) on all computer platforms and computer monitors.

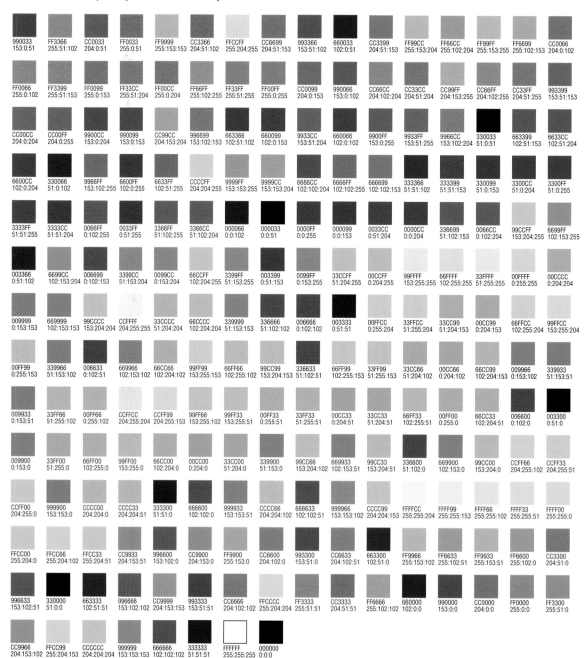